HARR

Marketing a
Service for Profit

Marketing a Service for Profit

A PRACTICAL GUIDE TO KEY SERVICE MARKETING CONCEPTS

GREG CLARKE

IN ASSOCIATION WITH

Marketing

KOGAN
PAGE

To Moni

First published in 2000

Kogan Page Limited
120 Pentonville Road
London
N1 9JN
UK

Kogan Page Limited
163 Central Avenue, Suite 2
Dover
NH 03820
USA

British Library Cataloguing in Publication Data

A CIP record for this book is available from the British Library.

ISBN 0 7494 1919 9

Typeset by Jean Cussons Typesetting, Diss, Norfolk
Printed and bound in Great Britain by Clays Ltd, St Ives plc

Contents

Acknowledgements

My thanks to Dave Woolf for creating and producing the cartoons. I would also like to thank Dennis Mellers for reading the draft manuscripts and for providing such positive feedback and useful comments about the content. I am also indebted to the various editors at Kogan Page for their patience!

Introduction

'The secret of getting ahead is getting started.' (Mark Twain)

If your business is totally service based, if you provide facilities for use by customers, or if you provide a level of service to your customer along with goods or any type of 'product', this book is for you. It is hoped that the book will also provide an interesting and useful adjunct to more formal text books for anyone studying marketing or business studies at any level.

Marketing a Service for Profit is not a text book of theories; it is a handbook of practical marketing concepts, techniques and strategies needed for success. Every attempt has been made by the author to help the reader lift the ideas and techniques from the page, rather than trying to just set them down in print. By the end of the book you will have not only gained a good grasp of proven marketing concepts and techniques that apply to marketing a service, but also be in a position to selectively employ them for profit. *Key points* are identified at each relevant stage and *Action points* start you moving in the right direction.

The only way to ensure the long term survival and success for a business is not only to work *in* it with determination, but also to work *on* it with care. Many commercial organizations are technically very good at what they do, but they are not always so good at informing and convincing people how good they are, or could be, given a chance. As a customer of many different services yourself, you know when you have received good service, and what it feels like to receive poor service or for your expectations not to have been met. Some service-based businesses are unfortunately high on hype in their advertising or promotional literature, or in what they say in order to persuade the customer to buy. Others appear to have perhaps lost their way strategically, or – worst of all – appear not to care about their customers.

Your business may not be represented by any of the above examples, yet you are seeking ways to improve performance: perhaps by finding more – and better quality – customers; or by improving your margins and thus increasing your profits; or by strategically altering the way you do things so that your customers come back time and again and appreciate what you do for them, at a price that is sensible for you.

This book is intended to provide you with a straightforward, pragmatic guide to understanding and implementing good marketing practice, in order to help you achieve success in your commercial activity, along with the rewards which success can bring. It sets out to help you improve the performance of your service business, to improve the quality of your marketing, to understand and avoid mediocrity in the service element of your firm's activities, and perhaps avoid failure caused by otherwise unexpected reasons.

If you are already running a business, you will know what the marketplace is like 'out there'. Customers can be elusive, and even when you have found them they can be fickle! If you are thinking of starting up, you will realize that if you do not have a customer, then you do not have a business! You need a market – a collection of customers – and you need to establish a successful route to that market. Starting up might be compared to learning to drive, or getting to grips with a personal computer; there seems to be so much to do and to think about while you are doing it, before you can even contemplate success! But just like driving a car or becoming computer literate, the skill of marketing a service comes with actually doing it. From the knowledge and understanding you gain in applying the tips and proven techniques described here, you can be confident that you will find ways that work for you and that you will be ready to spot opportunities and be able to capitalize on them.

1

A way of looking at things

'If you have a pound and I have a pound and we exchange pounds, you still have a pound and I still have a pound. But if you have an idea and I have an idea and we exchange ideas, you now have two ideas and I now have two ideas.'

Power in the commercial world has irreversibly shifted. Commercial power is no longer vested in the means of production, it lies now with 'the idea' and the control of the idea. The factory owner, mill owner and mine owner who were once powerful in times of shortage of supply are now being superseded by people who create systems, processes, intellectual property – and services.

Exponents of 'New Era Economics' maintain that all commercial transactions are service based, or rapidly becoming so. Whereas mass production gave customers an element of choice at relatively low cost, mass customization is providing customers with exactly what they want at a reasonable price because there is no wastage on the part of the producer. The communications revolution is turning goods producers into service providers and services into experiences. The growth in Internet e-commerce and specialist mail order business is bringing producers of goods into direct relationship with their customers. One effect of this is to enable the producer to respond rapidly to provide what the customer wants and react swiftly to changing market conditions. It moves the relationship with the customer to the beginning of the business process, instead of it forming part of the traditional sales transaction at the end. Previously held ideas of the 'flow' of goods: production/distribution/sales, are being turned upside-down as the commercial world moves further into a customer-led pattern of: sales/production/distribution. This is how service businesses have always operated. 'Customer relationship selling' became a recent vogue within companies producing goods; service companies have been operating 'customer relationship selling' for centuries. Now it is necessary for most businesses to place the emphasis upon understanding how to run a service business, within a predominantly service economy.

The word 'services' tends to be bundled up into the generic word 'products' as a catch-all description of business output. However, the word 'product' usually conjures the thought of something solid and tangible and is often used instead of the word 'goods', as when used in 'products and services', instead of referring to 'goods and services'. Goods and/or 'products' in this sense are tangible, solid things that can be seen, and upon which quality can be assessed before purchase. Services cannot be described that way. Services are intangible. Their quality cannot be assessed until after a commitment has been made to pay for them. When we are referring to services, it may, therefore, be useful to avoid the word 'product' altogether, in the colloquial use of that word.

Services cannot be 'seen' in the same way as a solid, tangible item. The influence of the visual media – television and print – has brought about the 'Visual Age' in which we live; an Age that is also inhabited by so many marketing people. The demands of the Visual Age, the visual image and, therefore, the visual advertisement, have dominated much marketing activity simply by sheer volume.

Is this why marketing is commonly interpreted as being just advertising?

The need for such relentless advertising attention to industrial and consumer goods has been brought about, not surprisingly, by manufacturing industry's need to sell its tangible industrial and consumer goods to unknown customers. In a world where there was demand for industrial and consumer goods that were in short supply, there was the need to convey the news that products were available, where and how they could be obtained, and at what price. Increasing competition within the supply side has changed the function of the advertisement, beyond the delivery of that original communication/news message. Emphasis is now placed on the 'unique selling proposition' (USP), the feature or features that distinguish one company's offering over another. These features are often now described in terms of the benefits they might convey to the customer, and advertising these days is generally centred on portraying the benefits to customers at whom the tangible industrial and consumer goods are aimed.

The need for this volume of 'Visual Age' advertising of goods may be the reason why scant attention has been paid to understanding the professional marketing of services. This is despite the fact that, as we are told, over 75 per cent of the UK's GNP arise from 'invisible' exports! Should the Gross National Product be renamed 'Gross National Service Sales (plus some Goods)'?

Long before the age of consumer goods and modern 'marketing', society was serviced by people. People provided services: tradespeople, artisans, merchants, porters, drivers, shopkeepers, bankers, stonemasons, washerwomen, millers, travelling actors, etc. These were the customers for whom many goods were made, to enable them to ply their trades. Consumer goods now enable us to do for ourselves many of the jobs previously sent out.

Many goods can perhaps be described as facilitating items; that is, they are bought in order that we can do some particular job or undertake a particular activity. Television and radio enter our homes so that we do not have to go out to seek entertainment. Cars enable us to see to our own transport needs. Yet it is as though society, full of consumer goods and status objects, is now turning again to the service provider to fulfil a sense of completeness, or to give meaning to a material age. Is it not ironic that many advertisers now stress the service element that accompanies the purchase of the products they are promoting, rather than the product itself? USP is rapidly coming to mean 'universal service promise' since there is sometimes little of a tangible nature to differentiate one make of product from its competitor and the customer wants more perceived value for money and more personal attention.

At best, however, services tend to be included only as a sort of adjunct to business, and always come second, as in the expression: 'products and services'. At worst, the functional and strategic needs of the service organization are by-passed altogether. If you are in a service industry, or looking to enter one, you would not be alone if you are left wondering how to interpret the plethora of business planning materials and marketing models generally available. It is not unusual to find that the general systems promoted by organizations, business books, banks and other financial institutions, are offered in a business language that has been handed down from our manufacturing heritage. For example, it is difficult to relate the needs of your service-based business to business planning spreadsheets formatted for the production, distribution and sale of widgets. Business planning advice, sales forecasting and reporting systems, and all manner of commercial calculations invariably pre-suppose that a business sells goods, widgets and things, even though manufacturing is now a minority economic activity. After all, things are easy to visualize and count; their components can be measured and accounted for; their distribution and cost of sales can be clearly identified in accounting terms. Such a nebulous concept as a service cannot be quantified for accountancy purposes, except as a cost rather than as a profit centre.

We do not seem to have yet established financial reporting systems within which service can be objectively valued or expressed. It has taken the professional world a long time to start to come to terms with the need to value a brand name or trade mark, yet here is where the real modern wealth lies.

Is it possible that the power of a brand lies in the service it provides for the customer?

Attempts are still made to constrain service marketing within the 'product' mould; to make service marketing fit models and systems that were designed when power and financial might rested with the means of production. The received wisdom and tendency throughout commerce is to describe everything offered by a business as being 'product'. Yet, we often experience a feeling of unease at this generalization, recognizing that some things that are 'produced' are not actually the core 'products' in which value is embodied, but simply outcomes of a process that is of itself hard to define. The process is hard to define because it is intangible and nebulous and we would much rather think in terms of solid, tangible goods that we can count.

What, for example, is 'produced' by your accountant? Is it just another bill for you to pay? Or is it your annual accounts? Or the tax savings? Or your compliance with regulation? Perhaps it is knowledge and understanding of the performance of your business, which will enable you to make strategic decisions? Or is it the advice he or she provides? Whatever your accountant produces, it is not just the paper it is written on. Perhaps that is just an interim product, or outcome, of an on-going business relationship. Perhaps it is the *relationship* that is the accountant's product, and everything else is a consequence of that relationship.

Buyer behaviour is becoming empowered by awareness and ease of choice, and buyers now have the technology to facilitate that choice. Quite a number of buying decisions no longer have to be weighed, only taken. Industries that have thrived on taking their cut as the middle-man for a poorly informed customer will need to redefine their mission, and reassess the core values they are offering, if they are not to be squeezed by severe cost-cutting and ever-shrinking margins in fiercely competitive markets that are currently based upon price alone.

Consider the industry of insurance broking. Insurance brokers offer a portfolio of 'products' from insurance companies and generally see pricing as their main weapon in trying to gain business, yet just undercutting equivalent quotes from rivals does not bring into the customer's reckoning all the service that the broker provides. If service is not at the centre of the broker's business policy, it is perhaps not surprising that most customers will concentrate on the price element of their arrangements, and buy direct from whichever supplier is currently cheapest in the market. Selling purely on price is rarely the best option for any long term business unless it is part of a wider, well thought out, marketing strategy. This applies particularly to insurance brokers who are selling other companies 'products', competing with every other broker dealing in the same commodity, while the vastly reduced costs of Internet trading and e-commerce are ready to overtake them all.

It is no wonder the broking industry has experienced such tough times, where the only perceived route to profit is now by way of merger or acquisition. One wonders what will happen when there is no one left to merge with or acquire! Perhaps the broking industry, like most other 'middle-men', commission-based service businesses, has to seriously consider whether it has dug itself into a hole. Their customers now have the technology to access a world of information and are no longer ill-informed – they can choose for themselves, arrange for themselves, and claim for themselves.

COMMENT

- Serious strategic problems can arise when a predominantly service industry tries to force itself to fit the received wisdom of the 'everything must be classed as product' mould.
- Is there an assumption that only tangible things have real value? Tangibility is easier to conceptualize than an intangible relationship and easier to place a monetary value on, but it also enables direct price comparison against competitors' tangible outputs.
- Many customers are naturally wary of any sales process and especially so if they – and service to them – are not at the centre of the transaction.

Banks and commission-led service businesses are vulnerable to opinion that they 'do not really earn their money', particularly as much of what they actually do is out of sight of the customer. Earnings for insurance brokers, travel agents, estate agents, etc still predominantly arise from commission on sales for 'products' that you could perhaps buy direct yourself. It is relevant to note that pricing of professional services is usually based on time, rather than commissions. Thus the accountant, solicitor, dentist, and even the golf pro, are each held in esteem as providing a valued service.

Perhaps if more insurance brokers marketed the value to be gained from a relationship with them as fee-based risk assessors and advisors, the industry might find new doors opening to ways of respectable and respected profits.

The demise of the travel agent is predicted by many, as the popular use of technology and the Internet enables direct booking of business flights and straightforward package holidays already promoted on the Web and teletext. As with the example described above, if the service provided by the travel agent is not at the centre of the marketing plan, it is perhaps not surprising that many people will concentrate on the price element of their arrangements and buy direct from whichever supplier is currently cheapest in the market.

Estate agents are already under threat from alternative channels through which people can choose, view, and buy property. Financial service products are just a telephone call away. Computers are bought direct, by mail order. Competing on price alone rarely provides the security of customer loyalty needed by a service business to enable it to confidently plan for the long term. As soon as a cheaper supplier enters the market, there is no reason for customers to remain loyal to their previous service provider. As indicated above, serious strategic problems can be generated within service industries by over-commitment to the 'product' concept, and consequent assumptions made about pricing, in a rapidly changing commercial environment.

Individual business failures are often described as having been unexpected and are sometimes even reported as spectacular crashes. In reality, very few are sudden events, although it may be only at the last minute that impending disaster suddenly dawns on the management or business owner. The causes of most failures are usually there, just waiting to effect themselves; they creep up to inevitably fill holes in inadequate planning and wishful thinking! Comments are heard about 'the poor state of the market', 'the soft market', or the general lack of work 'out there'. Mediocrity in returns can be hard to recognize and deal with and learning from experience often means that too much valuable time and money have been irretrievably lost.

As a wise man once said, 'Experience is what you gain just after you need it!'

Before experiencing difficulties and having to learn from expensive mistakes, perhaps we can seek knowledgeable solutions to our anticipated problems. The question is, from where should we seek answers? Specifically, services are to do with people, and successful marketing is all about satisfied people. Understanding the psychology of business/customer relationships is vital to successful marketing of services.

If you ask an accountant for a solution to a problem, do not be surprised when the answer comes back in accountancy terms from a financial viewpoint. Likewise, ask an engineer to solve a problem and he or she will find an engineering solution. Many attempts have been made to define the science of business: accountancy for the science of finance and bookkeeping; operations research for efficient manufacturing processes; economics for the understanding of supply and demand, etc. Science can also describe – to the nth degree – the chemistry of a water molecule. We believe science tells us everything we need to know about a molecule of H_2O – yet there is nothing in all of science to tell us that water is wet!

Water is wet only because we feel it is wet. It is the interaction between us and water that ascribes the characteristic of 'wetness'. It is marketing that brings that same added dimension of human experience to the science of business, and it is the marketing of services that may yet prove the deciding factor in the fight against mediocrity in financial performance for many businesses, as well as in the war against the decline that is anticipated for many middle-man industries.

So, how do you go about assessing the needs for your business? And where do you look for the right sort of marketing solutions that are suitable for your service business needs? I hope the following chapters guide you well.

2

What is a service?

'The most valued things in business aren't things.'

Chapter 1 drew a distinction between the tangible nature of goods and the intangibility of services. This distinction has been incorporated into some of the attempts that have been made by others to define what a service is. For example, 'A service is an activity or benefit that one party can offer to another that is essentially intangible and does not result in the ownership of anything. Its production may or may not be tied to a physical product' (Kotler and Armstrong, 1991). Other authors on the subject have likewise tried to define services, with varying degrees of lucidity. The Confederation of British Industry (CBI) classes as a service industry any business that is not involved in manufacturing, house building or construction. However, it is not the aim of this book to enter into semantics. Suffice to say there is no easy, all-encompassing nor concise definition of a service.

Perhaps it is more important to be aware of what *your customers* consider *their* definition of service to be and how your business is going to fulfil that perception.

Perhaps it is also time to look positively at the nature of services, rather than simply saying that they are not goods. Fundamentally, many businesses today are perhaps better described as 'facilities'. These are commercial offerings that are not goods, yet they seem to fall short of qualifying as services in our innate judgement of what a service is. Equipment, systems and processes are made available

for use by customers and there is very little, if any, human interaction between supplier and customer. To an extent, people use the word 'utilities' to cover electricity, gas, and water supplies, but this term has started to drop from the language, perhaps as a result of privatization of those industries and the modern pre-occupation with commercial 'product' and 'services'. Telecommunications, including the Internet, could conceivably be described as 'utilities' but this stretches the definition of that word as they are not yet part of the fabric of building construction in the way that electricity, gas and water are. Telecommunications, the Internet, railways, buses, libraries, cinemas, electricity, gas and water are all examples of facilities that are currently classed as services. There are a great many such businesses, providing customers with services (facilities) that are based more upon customer interaction with machinery, equipment and electronics than on personal interaction between people.

For the purposes of this book, 'services' can accommodate both people-based services and the provision of tangible facilities that provide services. But the time is perhaps approaching when we need a new mind-set; one that allows business processes and their outputs to be more accurately described as goods, facilities and services, instead of just goods and services. Certainly the basis for investment decisions and the marketing processes required can be very different, according to which of these three classifications is being considered.

CHARACTERISTICS OF SERVICES

We can, however, usefully consider those components that differentiate services from goods and that require detailed inspection and understanding. Intangibility is certainly one dimension of a service, meaning that a service cannot be touched, heard, smelt, tasted or seen. In the case of facilities, we certainly experience the equipment and the facilities are tangible, yet the service we obtain remains intangible. Likewise, we might see someone receiving a service, but that is not the same as seeing the service itself.

A customer cannot detect a service through any of the five senses, yet service will be experienced; that is, the customer will feel well (or badly) served. Indeed, a service has to be experienced before any judgement about its quality can be made at all, and that judgement will be based solely upon the customer's subjective opinion. This leads us to the realization that, other than its intangibility, three other crucial observations about a service are: the customer is involved in it; it is consumed while it is being provided; and only the customer can be the arbiter of its quality.

The fact that time can elapse between the production of goods and their subsequent purchase/use means that the processes of production by the producer and consumption by the customer are separate from one another. They can be separated in time and space and are, therefore, described as being separable. Whereas the production and subsequent purchase/use of goods are two distinct activities, the provision of a service requires the involvement of the customer throughout. Services are thus described as being inseparable. They cannot be produced at one location at a time most convenient to the producer, and then transported and/or stored for consumption when required by the customer at a later time. Implicit in the delivery of a service is the recognition that a service is consumed while it is being provided. Services cannot be stored and carried forward for sale at later date. This is usually described by marketing people as the perishability of services, although the concept of transience might describe it better. The concept is not one of the diminishing quality of an object, as implied by the term perishability, but that of an experience that remains whole but exists only for a particular period in time. For example, the opening night of a play cannot be repeated in the same theatre, nor can passengers join an aircraft once the flight has started.

The customer may buy, or book in advance, the right to a service process, such as a railway season ticket for future journeys, or an appointment for legal advice from a solicitor. In the first instance, the season ticket is purchased in advance of the planned journeys. In the second, the solicitor may be paid quite some time after the advice has been received. However, these two examples still both exemplify inseparability and transience as the overall service has simply been divided into two stages: the service provided at the point of sale or booking; and the service (facility) to be provided by the actual rail journeys or to be experienced at the meeting with the solicitor.

Because of the transient nature of a service, the management of the demand for a service – and the marketing methods required to achieve sustainable quality of service – are more crucial than those needed for the sale of goods. The service provider has to operate in tune with the peaks and troughs of immediate demand. For example, once a car ferry has left port, no further passengers can be booked on it. A sudden surge in demand at the quayside a few minutes later cannot be dealt with by that particular ferry. The marketing trick is to have filled the ferry profitably with happy customers and have made provision for the continuing demand! The service trick is to obtain all the possible repeat bookings from satisfied customers who wish to make similar future trips. Similarly, if we consider the provision of professional services, once all of the day's appointment slots in the professional's diary have been booked, there is no further time to see another client within normal hours that day.

In the case of goods, purchase generally conveys ownership, or acquisition of title, to the buyer. The quality of the goods can be inspected, measured or evaluated by the prospective customer prior to purchase, (although it is from the transference of ownership and subsequent use of goods that the customer assesses their 'merchantable quality' and 'fitness for the purpose'). However, services are *experienced* by the customer as they are being provided, rather than becoming *owned*. The buyer is purchasing a right to a service process or facility, such as the use of a hotel room for the night, the use of a telephone, or to have their office cleaned.

By their very nature the quality of services will be variable, and this is compounded by the fact that each customer will use their own subjective opinion to judge the quality of the service according to their personal experience of it. Because of the relationship nature of a service, much depends upon the person delivering the service and how the relationship is managed by that person. The monitoring and control of quality standards is difficult in these circumstances. Whilst goods are replicated to provide consistency and predictability through ever more exacting design and material specifications, services are appreciated when they are flexible enough to change to meet the specific needs of each individual customer. During repeat sales, customers will expect consistency and predictability of standards in the service provided, or an improvement in those standards, related to the perceived quality of their original experience.

The need for flexibility from the service provider may initially be a cause for concern to the customer, who may well perceive a definite risk of disappointment or financial loss as a consequence of the relationship. As the quality of a service only becomes evident whilst it is being received, after the customer has committed to paying for it, the customer has to trust the service provider to deliver on their word. Even a small change in what has been promised by the service provider can result in major dissatisfaction on the part of the customer. Closure of a shop during its stated opening hours can cause serious annoyance amongst potential customers at that time and will create uncertainty in their minds as to whether the shop will be open if they try to visit again. A poor product may be tolerated or even tried again, but poor service is rarely given the opportunity to be repeated. Where provision of service is coupled with the purchase of goods, loss of trust caused by poor service can totally undermine future sales of all goods from that supplier.

SERVICE MACHINES

As described in the above references to facilities, business may use machines to provide elements of service. For example, Automated Teller Machines (ATMs) are provided by banks, building societies and some supermarkets to handle many of the straightforward financial transactions and information needed by busy customers. From the business point of view they represent low cost delivery channels for high volumes of transactions. The success of these machines rests on the trust placed in them by customers and the customer's estimation of their own ability to understand and use them. If the machine seems too difficult to operate, appears likely to behave in an unexpected way, facilitates fraud against the customer, causes mistakes on the customer's account, or places the customer's personal safety at risk, then the machine will not be trusted and will not be used. It is estimated that a quarter of the population does not trust this type of technology. There is also belief that banks are purposely 'deselecting' certain categories of customer, in other words, those who perhaps need banking services more than the banks need them, those who do not maintain sizeable accounts or do not take up the more profitable 'products' offered by the bank.

Whilst the availability and convenience of 'user-friendly' machines (facilities) may be welcomed by many customers, the very fact that a machine is used in a service capacity to replace a human being to provide the same service may be viewed with scepticism and/or disdain by some customers. Some people reserve the title 'service' only for when caring attention is paid to them by another person, otherwise it is termed self-service. The main benefit attributable to the use of machines is that they can save time for the busy customer, whether in the example of a banking context as above, or on the petrol station forecourt for self-service of fuel, or in any other routine transaction where something is dispensed.

Is saving time through the use of 'service machines' the positive provision of a service, or is it merely the removal of the possibility of aggravating slowness on the part of sales assistants?

As a society we now have access to a great many 'services' that are really only classified as services because they are patently not tangible goods. The term 'facilities' is offered here as a definable third category of business offering, describing the process where we use equipment, machinery or systems whose ownership does not pass to us. It might then be easier to distinguish between goods, facilities and services, and the word 'service' could be reserved for when we feel that we have been 'served' rather than perhaps just 'processed' and the whole concept of 'real service' might not appear to be so undermined. Rail, sea and air travel are examples of facilities we use only for the duration that we need them. These facilities can be provided with little or no personal contact between the customer and the facility provider. Tickets can be dispensed from machines, a screen shows departure arrangements and the transport is provided for our journey. The serving of in-flight meals, or assistance rendered by cabin staff, etc would thus count as service, whereas the flight itself is a facility. A simple definition might be that only people can provide service, and all equipment is classed as facility.

People do not always want service; sometimes all that is wanted is the use of the facilities. The facility of the Internet and its World Wide Web is relished by many who delight in using new technology and who can use their knowledge to gain the benefit of saving time. The Internet offers such people a great many opportunities for business transactions. Others may view with suspicion and/or apprehension the prospect of conducting any business over the Internet until it becomes totally risk-free, that is, a preference is exercised whereby business is conducted with other people, not with a 'machine'.

As described above, provision and consumption of a service are inseparable, and a service is consumed as it is being provided. These factors imply the active involvement of the customer in a relationship with the service provider. Time is an integral dimension of the process. The active involvement of the customer in receiving a service means that, for services, time is of the essence and timeliness is invariably a vital consideration in the customer's evaluation of the quality of the service.

TIME, QUALITY AND CONVENIENCE

Because of the customer's transient participation and involvement in the service process, the customer is assessing quality throughout the time of its delivery – before, during and after the point of sale. An organization's marketing message may influence customer expectations, but the organization's own description of the quality of its service remains only its own description of it; customers will decide the real quality for themselves, from their own experience. This is particularly true when a service is provided on a one-to-one basis, such as with professional advice, banking, call-centres, retailing, consultancy, etc. To some extent the customer's perception of quality can be influenced by other customers, and the presence of other customers receiving the service at the same time can be part of the service process – watching a play in an otherwise empty theatre would be a strange and less enjoyable experience than being part of a theatre audience.

The process of providing services for many customers simultaneously is of course fraught with potential problems caused by the sheer numbers of people, such as delays, queuing, public safety and personal security. In this sort of environment it is easy for the service provider to forget or ignore the needs of individuals and possibly to side-line the feelings customers are experiencing about the service as they live through it. It is also often in this sort of context that what is conventionally classed as a service might be better described as a facility.

Customer expectations are rising. People are gaining awareness of choice – and the facilities to exercise that choice – more conveniently than ever before. Customers are often prepared to pay for convenience as long as the perceived value for money and/or the benefits to be gained from that convenience outweigh any perceived risk.

Thus customers of a launderette may operate the washing and drying machines themselves, either for direct control of the quality of the process to reduce risk of damage to their washing, or to save the expense of paying for a service wash. The business offer here is limited to that of facility, as there is nothing in the transaction that might be described as service. The convenience aspect will then be vested in the location and opening times of the launderette, along with any benefits perceived in not having to own and run their own washing machine. On the other hand, if they feel they can trust the staff to look after their clothes and fabrics, customers may consider the cost of the service wash well worth the time and effort that it saves them. This choice may be made whether they own a washing machine or not, or if the items to be washed are too bulky for their own domestic machine. In the case of the service wash, the convenience aspect is vested in the ability to simply deliver the washing to the launderette and collect it later. There is also recognition that in this case a service has been rendered. The location of the launderette and its opening times are still considerations, but may not be such critical factors to the customer as if they were using the facilities themselves.

Because the provision of a service is so inextricably bound up with the relationship between the customer and the service provider, human factors are of vital importance for successful transactions. Service providers achieve far greater success if every member of their staff is a 'people person'. That is, staff have intuitive understanding of human priorities within the commercial transaction and there is the possibility of immediate rapport with the customer's needs. The process of selling within this environment becomes the process of listening and giving credence to what the customer is saying. Likewise, the sincerity of the salesperson is being constantly assessed by the customer and will make the difference between mediocre business performance and real success. Saying 'Have a nice day' sounds hollow and almost cynical when spoken by someone who does not really care whether you have a nice day or not! People like to buy from other people who care about what they are selling and who appreciate the customer's viewpoint. Having a passion for what you do has a recognizable value in the service industry.

KEY POINTS

- Services are intangible – they cannot be identified through the five senses, yet they are experienced.
- There is no adequate overall or concise definition of a service, except that offered by the customer.
- Perhaps we should change the conventional wisdom by replacing 'goods and services' with 'goods, facilities and services'.

- The customer is intimately involved in the provision of a service – it is based on a relationship.
- A service is consumed while it is being provided – time is a vital dimension of a service.
- Only the recipient of a service can be the arbiter of its quality – after the commitment has been made to pay for it.
- The customer has to risk putting their trust with the service provider – there is none of the predictability associated with tangible goods, which can be pre-inspected or returned if found to be faulty.
- Quality will inevitably vary from occasion to occasion – dependant on both the provider and the recipient. In some cases the quality of the experience is dependent upon a number of customers being involved simultaneously.
- Services are a 'people thing' – requiring specialist skills and the management of interaction.
- Successful service businesses have a passion for what they do. They employ people who are people-orientated and who have a vocation for what the business provides.
- The purchase of a service does not transfer ownership or title to the buyer, although it may convey rights.

SERVICES AND GOODS

It is important for businesses to understand what exactly the customer is buying as opposed to what they think they are selling. The pizza restaurant provides an environment in which its customers can buy, consume and enjoy its products. The pizza delivery firm is perhaps providing the convenience of delivery first, with the pizza itself being of secondary consideration to that convenience – perhaps pizza was chosen for lunch, instead of burgers, only because the pizza could be delivered, whereas burgers normally are not. This point will be explored in more detail later on, but it raises here an example of a service that is inextricably linked to a tangible product.

Sometimes a service has to be provided in order to facilitate the purchase of goods. As in the example of pizza delivery, the delivery service must take place before transfer of ownership of the pizza can take place. The service may or may not be provided by the supplier of the goods. Consider, for example, the process of

'I know I left our company's service around here somewhere!'

buying a house. Before ownership of the house can be transferred, it may be necessary to arrange a mortgage and appoint a solicitor to handle the conveyancing. Further, the mortgage supplier will want the property adequately insured, and the solicitor will expect a measure of service from the vendor's solicitor. In these situations the customer is buying the service because they have to, not necessarily because they want to. Because of this, customers may be more critical and sensitive to pricing issues, especially if their choice of service provider is limited or they are already working to a tight timescale or budget. The issue of needs versus wants will be raised again later on. The relevant point here is that it can be a major factor in how the customer views the entire purchasing transaction; whether the customer is already positively or negatively inclined towards the service provider at the outset.

Monopolies disallow choice, and for most goods, apart from some pharmaceuticals, people can usually elect to find an alternative solution to their problem or do without certain goods if they are not happy over quality. Whilst a customer might choose not to buy particular goods, for some services they may have no such viable alternative solution available. Some rail commuters are obliged to continue using low quality train services, and some disgruntled householders have no choice but to accept fluoridation of their water supply.

Of course, the act of purchasing most goods is coupled with an element of service, as in the case of the pizza restaurant mentioned above. Timeliness, pleasantness and concern for the customer's needs are always appreciated during any transaction, whether the customer is a commercial/industrial buyer or whether customers are individuals buying for themselves. Retailing is considered to be a service industry, as are other 'middle-men' operations as mentioned in Chapter 1.

A business offer may comprise pure service, such as freight handling or courier work, dry cleaning, hairdressing and car valeting, or a mixture of service and facility such as a children's day nursery, nursing or retirement home. Alternatively, as in the example of pizza delivery, the service provided may be the vital element of a sales offer based on the transfer of ownership of goods. Further examples of this might be car repairs where new parts are fitted, or a post office for buying a tax disk for the car. At the other end of a continuum, which has pure services at one end and a mixture of service and goods in the middle, are examples of business offers that are enhanced by the addition of a service, to add value to goods that could otherwise be easily purchased on their own. Someone buying a computer may prefer to buy from a supplier offering an installation service or a 'help-desk' service, or from one who offers both of these additional services.

These added-on services may or may not be 'free'. In an age apparently dominated by accountants, customers are experiencing service levels cut to the bone in the mistaken belief on the part of suppliers that minimum cost means maximum profit. Both domestic and business customers may be satisfied for the extra cost to be included in the higher price of what is now a complete 'package' of goods and service, since what is being bought along with the goods is convenience and/or the transfer of risk should anything go wrong. In either case the customer may be willing to pay a premium for installation as they may not have the time or perhaps the skill to install the equipment properly, and cannot be held liable for incorrect installation. Likewise, the help-desk idea will appeal to an employer whose staff can use it to learn how to make the most from the new computer facility and minimize potentially expensive mistakes on it. Domestic customers may similarly appreciate a period of 'hand-holding' as they get to grips with the technology they have purchased.

It is possible, however, that competition from rival suppliers forces such added service elements to be given free of charge, either as an extra benefit to entice the type of customer who would appreciate the offer, or because provision of the service (or facility) element has become an accepted norm from major suppliers in the market. An example of this latter point is 'free' Internet access now available with the purchases from particular suppliers. The cost of Internet access is recovered by the service (facility) provider from the telecoms (facility) provider whose business has been increased, instead of being charged by the service provider directly to the customer.

Services and facilities can also be supplemented by adding on a further service element. An hotel can choose whether to provide its customers with room service. The availability of room service may be expected by customers in a very expensive hotel, but it becomes an arbitrary factor decided by management in the mid-priced range establishment. Where the availability of room service is seen as adding value, in order to be able to charge a higher room rate, or as a feature that distinguishes that hotel from its competitors and encourages trade, then the service will be incorporated into the total business offer. The distinction between service and facility is again applicable here. The hotel might offer room service as an extra service, whereas provision of a swimming pool offers an additional facility.

KEY POINTS

- What are customers actually buying when the sales offer comprises both goods and services?
- Do a firm's customers need its service, or do they voluntarily want it? This can have implications on how the service is inclined to be viewed by potential customers.
- Timeliness, pleasantness, and a concern for the customers' needs are always appreciated.

- Distinctions may need to be drawn between 'service' and 'facility'.
- The route to maximum profit is not through minimum cost.

ACTION POINTS

- How are your customers inclined to view the service you offer? Find out!
- Is your business purely service? Is the purchase of goods from another supplier dependent upon the service you provide, or do you provide a mixture of goods and services? These factors will affect your strategy for finding and keeping customers. Analyze your business in these terms and rethink your strategies in terms of what your customers do, rather than what you do.
- Can you add on a service to your existing business offer, to encourage customers to come to you and/or continue buying from you, or to increase your turnover and profit by selling an improved 'package' of benefits?
- Categorize your business into service (people) based and facilities based components. Does this affect your investment strategy? Does it affect your view of what market you are in?

CUSTOMER OR CONSUMER?

So far, the terms customer and consumer have been used almost synonymously, yet they may not be the same. If I make baked beans, it would be easy to think that my customer is 'the housewife'. But it isn't; it is the retailer. The retailer buys my beans from me, and then sells those beans on to my consumers, who are the retailer's customers. The pertinent point is that each party will have differing needs. For the consumer, the flavour of the beans may be all important, whereas perhaps what is important for my customer – the store – is that I deliver before 9.00 am (ie the service element of my business). So it can be when selling services, that we miss a step in our definition of who our customer is and thus perhaps miss a vital step in our business offer. Services are a 'people thing' and we do well to think through whether our customer and consumer are the same person, or two different people, even within the same organization.

As an example, imagine you are a Training Consultant discussing what you can offer to the Personnel Manager of another firm. Who is your customer? Is it the Personnel Manager, or perhaps the Personnel Director? You may say it is the company as a whole. But services are a 'people thing', so who is the person who is your customer? Certainly the Personnel Manager is the one you are dealing with, yet your 'customer' is perhaps really the Finance Director. After all, the only reason that a firm buys in any form of consultancy is to do with money. Either you are going to save them money, or you are going to make them money, or you are enabling them to transfer risk. Your selling points, then, are all to do with money and cost-effectiveness, and the custodian of the corporate cheque book is... the Finance Director! Of course, the Managing Director is the main player and may indeed be the true customer, in that he or she authorizes the consultant's fee, but it is worth remembering that he or she will take counsel from each member of the team, and first in line will be the Finance Director.

If you were the Training Consultant, it might be prudent to consider the Personnel Manager/Director as your consumer, the main person in the department you are proposing to directly assist, but the person who is either writing your cheque or under-writing the payment is the customer. Your fee may come out of the Personnel Department's budget, but that is allocated by the Board. When selling a service to another business, it is often useful to think through exactly how each Board Director/department will benefit from your involvement. In the case of training, the relevant department may increase productivity or improve its efficiency, which might then help other departments do their work better. The overall effect spreads beyond the individual who is being trained and beyond the realm of the Personnel Department – and always ends up with Finance, whether you have taken the trouble to sell-in your benefits to them or not!

A similar situation can arise if you are selling services to the public. It is easy to think of a household, or just the one person in it with whom you are dealing, as being the customer, but great care must be taken if two (or more) people live within the same house-hold. It will be essential that you satisfy the value criteria of both customer and consumer within the household, and that you have correctly identified what those criteria are. Consider a domestic heating gas service engineer carrying out a maintenance check on the system under the terms of a service agreement with a household. If, for the purpose of this example, we assume a 'traditional' family structure, then the lady of the house might view herself as a consumer while the man might see himself as the customer. One may rate the quality of the service in terms of whether the engineer seemed to know what he was doing, was polite, and cleaned up after himself, whereas the other may judge the work only on its technical aspects and be more critical of the cost.

KEY POINT

- The customer and the consumer may have very different needs and will, therefore, each require their own definition of quality to be satisfied.

ACTION POINTS

- Who is your customer and who is your consumer?
- Are they the same person or different people?
- How does this affect how you sell?

THE SERVICE ENVIRONMENT

When buying goods, customers usually have the opportunity to examine them fully before purchase and are generally aware of their rights to restitution in the event of the goods turning out to be faulty, not of merchantable quality or not 'fit for the purpose'. Consumer Law and the various Sale of Goods Acts and other regulations help to protect the public, although the maxim *caveat emptor* (let the buyer beware!) remains the underlying doctrine. When buying services, customers do not have the opportunity to examine what they are buying before the commitment has been made to pay for them. For this reason the *caveat emptor* doctrine is seen as less reasonable when applied to the purchase of services; it is not possible to return or exchange a service, and its transient nature means that the customer has to trust that the quality of the service is up to standard first time round.

Services available for purchase by the public are, therefore, likely to be the subject of specific legal control, or official or voluntary regulation within each type of service industry. For example, the Financial Services industry is now strictly controlled by law; the Civil Aviation Authority licences aircraft operators, the Advertising Standards Authority watches over the advertising industry and the Association of British Travel Agents (ABTA) is a trade body that sets standards for tour operators who offer their services for sale through travel agents. In UK banking, insurance and many other services, an Ombudsman exists to help consumers obtain restitution for shoddy or illegal work. The Law Society in the same way oversees the activities of the legal profession and can call solicitors to account on behalf of poorly served customers, and industry regulators have power over the recently privatized utilities.

It is because of the expected variation in service quality from a diversity of service providers that prospective customers look for coherent basic quality standards to be applied. In some sectors this is achieved by customers choosing to purchase only from service providers who can demonstrate that they comply with some form of external quality standard. Membership by the service provider of a trade association or other body that promotes a code of ethics can help to allay some of the fears their potential customers might otherwise have about variability of the quality of service to expect.

Changes within the economy and political arena can cause major shifts within the service industry. Deregulation of many public utility services has had a profound effect within these markets and has brought into the arena a larger number of smaller service providers where previously monopolies or near-monopolies had held sway. Monopolies are seen as being generally against the public interest and the introduction of competition is seen as a way of improving the quality of services while driving down prices.

Whilst these objectives may have been achieved in certain sectors of the service industry, such as perhaps telecommunications and radio broadcasting, it seems that sometimes the emphasis is placed too much on reducing prices, at the expense of service quality. An example could be seen in the deregulation of public bus service services. It was a complaint of bus user organizations that the new individual bus service operators vied with each other on price for the most lucrative routes and neglected rural routes, 'cross-country' routes, and less popular times of the day and night, all of which had been enjoyed to a greater extent by consumers before deregulation.

Ironically, the public may likely view poor service, or the absence of service altogether, as being indicative of a struggling, less-efficient business, rather than being a sign of a cost-effective successful one. This might be explained by considering bus services as really being bus facilities, since they offer little in the way of personal service. It is easy then to assume that a firm cannot afford to provide the facilities required.

As discussed earlier, service quality is by its nature variable and difficult to manage from the centre. It is not surprising that the service industry is, therefore, generally made up of a large number of small suppliers, where each supplier can more closely monitor and control the quality of their own service delivery and be flexible enough to match specific customer demands. For example, it is still the case today that 'Britain is a nation of small shop-keepers.' Although a few large retail chains appear to dominate the High Street – and there is a proliferation of out-of-town retail sites – it remains the case that around two-thirds of all UK retail businesses are single-outlet. Likewise, the vast computer services industry is comprised of a great many small-scale service providers, often employing only a handful of people or just a single person working as a consultant or on contract.

FINANCE, FUNDING AND CASH-FLOW

Whereas businesses manufacturing goods can require large amounts of capital investment, and this might also be true for services that provide facilities, such as transport or communications, a great many service businesses require only minimal capital. The implications arising from this are that services can be copied by competitors both easily and quickly. Consultancy or trade services are each in relatively low-cost entry markets and this is appealing to the individual operator who can very quickly emulate and possibly improve upon services originated by others.

Although some service providers have grown to sizeable proportions in terms of assets, financing of general facilities is often by way of leasing, rental or factoring and often little capital is required to start up in business – a recruitment agency essentially only needs office space and a telephone, a window cleaner just a ladder, bucket and leather. One implication of this is that financial appraisal and decision-making will be generally based more on direct profitability and cash-flow than on return on capital employed (ROCE) or balance sheet strength.

This also reflects the observations made in Chapter 1 concerning the suitability for services of many of the existing business planning materials and marketing models, which are traditionally designed for manufacturing and distribution of goods, where investment decisions are often centred on ROCE and balance sheet strength. The basis on which investment decisions for service providers has to be made is often thus considered to be as intangible and transient as the service itself! It is, therefore, hard to quantify a service in terms of measurable risk since so much depends upon the successful delivery of the service to each and every customer.

Proven track record, experience in the market, and commitment are all vital factors in considering whether timely repayment will be forthcoming on any investment or loan to a service provider. Even then, investors may seek to limit their risk to a particular project rather than to the service provider as an entity; film studios seek investors for each film, and commercial television seeks sponsors for individual programmes, rather than further investment in their corporate status. It is also not unknown for investors in companies to become disenchanted with a service provider whose output is based upon creativity or entertainment. A steady increase in the value of their investment can only be matched by regular or rising outputs from the service provider of ever more creative material, and this is rarely humanly possible.

Cash-flow is of vital importance for any business, but this is particularly true for service providers. Overtrading occurs when a business takes on more work than it has resources to deal with and can result in financial collapse no matter how profitable the venture. Indeed, in many cases the more successful the business is, the faster it goes bust.

Consider, for example, a highly profitable recruitment agency supplying temporary staff to other organizations. The temporary staff will usually require payment a week or fortnight in hand and certainly no later than the end of the month in which they are employed. However, it is probably not until the end of the month before the agency can raise its invoice to the customer. Even if the customer responds promptly and pays the agency's invoice within 30 days, it means that a 'black hole' is developing within the agency's cash flow as it recruits more and more temporary staff. In other words, the more contracts the agency has to fulfil, the more working capital is being sucked into the 'black hole' to pay wages, and the more cash it needs just to stay afloat. The situation becomes severely compounded if the customer takes 60 or 90 days to pay their invoice!

Controlling credit is thus a major consideration for many service providers, who have no possibility of retaining title or recovering goods from bad debtors. Credit control thus has to be a cornerstone of any business hoping to market a service for profit.

KEY POINTS

- Because services are intangible and transient, not allowing for examination prior to purchase, much of the service sector is subject to a great deal of legislation and internal regulation. Where such regulation may not exist, customers have to rely upon promises made at initial presentations. Failure to live up to the customers' subsequent expectations will severely damage the service provider's reputation and consequent ability to gain any further contracts or repeat business. (Because regulation tends to arise out of the need to control sharp practice or shoddy service that has already occurred, regulation arrives too late for many already dissatisfied customers, and potential new customers only remember the 'horror stories' they have heard, which add to their wariness, mistrust and suspicion).

- Customers generally prefer to deal with service providers who can demonstrate that they have voluntarily adopted an external quality standard or code of ethics to govern how they perform.

- National economic and political changes can have a major impact on how services are provided, and by whom.

- There are a great many small-scale service providers (whereas there are a smaller number of large scale manufacturers).
- Services can often be quickly and easily copied by competitors. If a distinction is drawn between services and facilities, and a firm relies only on providing facilities, then anyone providing similar or better facilities will gain market share.
- Funding decisions for many service providers may be project-based, or are more likely to be concerned with profitability and cash-flow forecasts than with ROCE or balance sheet calculations.
- Many service markets are low-cost entry and yet require increasing amounts of working capital. As such, funding methods may well need to concentrate on satisfying the demands of cash-flow to prevent overtrading.
- Credit control is essential for commercial success and must play a central role in any strategy designed to market a service for profit.

3

Practical marketing concepts

'The secret of getting started is breaking your complex overwhelming tasks into small manageable tasks, and then starting on the first one.' (Mark Twain)

The objectives of good marketing should be the cost-effective start-up and running of a profitable venture that has happy, smiling repeat customers serviced by competent and confident staff. Achieving this means that marketing has to be a customer-centred process carried out with passion and enthusiasm throughout the service provider's organization. Staff need to be empowered with concern for each customer's experience all the way through the transaction and beyond, to the memory of it. The service provided may be copied by others, but a unique reputation in the market-place can be built upon providing distinctive memories.

Having considered the special nature and characteristics of services, this chapter introduces you to some of the main marketing concepts, together with techniques for employing them to improve the profitable marketing of services. Marketing is not so much an activity as a process, undertaken by an organization as a whole. It is perhaps important to recognize that some sort of marketing happens whether it has been planned or not! The natural state of a business is to go bust, but hopefully it does not go bust and actually improves because its directors, proprietors and/or managers do the right things to it. It is thus useful to first understand the roles of manager and director or proprietor in the marketing process.

DEFINING ROLES IN THE MARKETING PROCESS

The role of the manager

The role of the manager within any organization is basically made up of three fundamental functions: planning, implementation, and control. Marketing a service for profit requires the same professional approach if the probability of success is to be maximized. Just trying out a new marketing idea without adequate planning or control can seriously affect a company's reputation if it goes wrong. From an understanding of the points covered in the preceding chapter, it is recognized that a service organization has to continually re-invent its reputation with every transaction with every customer and, therefore, cannot afford to risk leaving any bad memories in the minds of its customers.

The role of the director or proprietor

The role of the director or proprietor of a business is not only to ensure that the business is properly managed, but also to set and regulate the pace and direction of the business, and to protect it. The concepts of marketing vision and strategy, therefore, come into play in order to create the environment and climate in which plans may be laid, implemented and controlled.

Failure to set and regulate the pace of business growth in line with capability and achievable ambition is a very common cause of business collapse. If the business grows too slowly it does not generate enough profit, nor the all-important cash needed to remain viable. As previously described, services can usually be easily copied (and perhaps improved) by competitors, so it is common for one firm to stimulate demand and then find its potential customers being serviced by competitors, and a migration of its existing customers going the same way. If the business grows too quickly then overtrading can occur. Overtrading happens when the organization does not have enough funds to keep its business afloat. The business can be highly profitable, but if it does not have enough cash to pay its bills as they fall due, then it goes bust. For an example of this, see Chapter 2: Finance, funding and cash-flow. (To continue trading as a limited company knowing that the company is insolvent is a criminal offence under the Companies Act.)

For a service business, the term 'overtrading' might also be usefully applied within a quality context if the service provider is trying to deal with too many customers at once. Insufficient resources or facilities to meet demand will immediately cause dissatisfaction amongst a great many customers and result in loss of both reputation and, possibly, subsequent business. Inadequate staffing, or reliance upon staff who are inadequately trained to cope, will each result in severe quality problems as perceived by the customer, who will turn in future to a more reliable service provider or simply quit using that service altogether. It is recognized that if a business is prepared to drop its quality once, then it will more than likely do it again – and customers, who can have very long memories, may not be prepared to risk that. The smaller business is particularly dependent upon word-of-mouth advertising to gain new customers, but that same channel of communication can equally kill trade if the news is bad. It is also not uncommon to see owners of small businesses 'overtrading' either on their health or domestic relationships, or both.

Setting and regulating business

As with driving a car, sometimes the business can run at a steady pace for long distances, yet has to be prepared to slow down or speed up according to conditions and changes in direction. Setting and regulating the direction of the business requires a vision of where you want to be, awareness of how the land lies ahead, and knowing where you are now. Thus, goal-setting and strategic planning are vital parts of the marketing exercise and these are both based upon market intelligence and information.

'Knowing where you are now' comes from keeping records. It is an astonishing fact that an estimated two-thirds of all businesses that go bust do so because of inadequate record keeping! Directors or proprietors of successful businesses have their 'fingers on the pulse' at all times. They know that it is their role to work *on* the business, as well as *in* it. Apart from recording and analyzing financial amounts, the successful market-orientated business will also have detailed and up-to-date information to hand concerning its customers: who they are and who they are buying for; what they are buying; where they are and where they like to buy; how they buy, when they buy; and why they are buying. This information is crucial for the directors or proprietor to know if the organization as a whole is to have the benefit of knowing 'where it is now', that is, the starting point for the future. As will be seen in later chapters, all of this information plays a key part in determining how the business is to develop in terms of both direction and size.

As with driving your car, you do not generally set off without knowing your planned destination, nor without having some idea of the route and possible conditions along the way. The same applies to your business – what are the goals, what directions must be followed to achieve them, and how does the land lie in between?

Protecting the business usually comes down to meaning protecting reputation and/or share-holder value. Gaining, sustaining and improving customer confidence are all vital in these contexts and are fundamental aspects of the director's or proprietor's responsibilities. Because of their active involvement in the service transaction, customers need to know that their custom is valued by the service provider and that they are not being taken for granted.

On-going, properly structured and well thought-through public-relations activity can also help to make all the difference to the customer's perception of the company. For example, mergers and acquisitions in the services sector are often brought about as much by the need to enlarge the customer base as to rationalize facilities or gain economies of scale. If the former customers of either company feel that they have lost their traditional sense of service then the newly enlarged customer base, on which the merger or acquisition was based, can shrink alarmingly. Service customers will, wherever possible, 'vote with their feet'. If a marketing strategy is not put into place by the dominant company to positively retain all existing customers, at least until any change in direction of the new force has been carefully set in place, then all of the customers will feel that they are being expected to live through the pain and expected to suffer any consequent disruptions while things are being 'sorted out'. Notices apologizing for inconveniences or delays are not positive replacements to finding alternative temporary ways of providing good service and at best are only a damage limitation exercise.

Whilst the British nature has in the past been fairly tolerant in such circumstances, that environment is rapidly changing with the advent of ever more service providers becoming available and customers being prepared to exercise choice. Customer expectations – and cynicism – are rising all the time. Many potential customers are cynical about advertising claims and, given the choice, may well prefer to wait until a new service becomes established before patronizing it themselves. People are learning to anticipate that 'bugs' may need to be ironed out of new systems and are thus reticent about embracing new ideas and new offerings from unproven service providers.

There will always be a proportion of customers who want to be in the vanguard of new ideas, but the 'help-line' is not much use if it cannot be accessed, is always busy, and no-one is available to take the call. The advertising campaign is a mockery if customers feel they have been left stranded by an ill-prepared company. Those customers who are first to take the risk of switching to a new service provider are often severely disappointed by what they find and consequent media coverage of their anger and/or frustration is hardly good 'word of mouth' advertising for the potential customers who are expected to follow. Again, well-managed public relations can be of enormous assistance should disaster strike and a firm needs to ask for customers' continuing faith in its ability to provide the service.

KEY POINTS

- The role of the manager is to plan, implement the plan and control the plan and its implementation. The role of the director or proprietor is to set and regulate the pace and direction of the business, and to protect it.
- Businesses need to grow at varying rates, according to trading/financial conditions and changes in direction. Too rapid growth of the business can cause overtrading and possible collapse. Failure to set goals and control direction causes the business to lose its way. If there are no goal

posts, how do you know when you have scored? How can success, mediocrity or failure be measured without a definition of success?
- Failure to protect the reputation of the business is fatal for a service provider.
- Constant attention to positive public relations can help persuade new customers to try the service, and having an established positive identity/image really helps if a damage limitation exercise is called for.

ACTION POINTS

- Set achievable goals for short term, medium term and longer term growth. Financial goals are essential (as is the cash-flow necessary to achieve them). Support financial goal setting with quality-indicator goals, eg the percentage of turnover that comes from repeat custom; the number of congratulatory or 'thank you' letters you receive (and the number of complaints!); the number of customer referrals from existing customers to new ones (analysing responses to the question: 'How did you hear about our service?'), etc.
- Set up a positive public relations programme, using professional PR assistance. For many service businesses, this can be far more cost-effective and productive than a straight advertising campaign.
- Try phoning your own company's head office switchboard, help-line, or customer-care number, as if you were a customer. Do it now.

FEATURES, ADVANTAGES, BENEFITS – AND THE ULTIMATE BENEFIT

People do not buy products – they buy the benefits they expect to gain from them. This applies as much to services as to goods. Successful marketing, therefore, considers not what you are selling, but what the customer is buying. Consider the six nearest pubs to where you live. One will be extremely busy, while the other five are not. Yet all six are selling basically the same 'products': beer, lager, crisps, etc. In the busy one, however, customers are gaining atmosphere, ambience, hospitality, friendliness; perhaps the landlord has taken the trouble to remember your name. The beer may even be an extra penny a pint, but who cares? Customers are not there just for the beer – they could have provided that for themselves much cheaper from the supermarket. Pub products may be accounted for in terms of barrels, bottles and boxes, but they do not in themselves account for success for the licensee or his customers.

The question arises as to how to differentiate between features, advantages and benefits, since an understanding of what comprises a benefit will be key to successful marketing. The same principles apply to the service situation as to the purchase of goods. In order to demonstrate how a benefit is derived, imagine you are buying a car and the salesman says, 'I've just the car for you – it's an extra £100 but it has ABS brakes!' You may consider the offer, but dismiss it perhaps because you are not sure what ABS brakes are, you have never had them before, or you think the salesman is just trying to sell you a feature that you do not really want or need.

If the salesman goes on to describe the advantage of ABS brakes, 'This car has ABS brakes, which means that they help prevent skidding.' You may be impressed with the idea, but then try to recall for yourself the last time you did actually skid. Would these brakes have helped on that black ice? So you think to yourself, 'No, I don't need these extras. If I'm careful while I'm driving, I've saved myself £100.'

You will have interpreted that the salesman has implied that driving might be safer with ABS brakes, or he may indeed have pointed out the benefit of safety as a result of having ABS brakes: 'This car has ABS brakes, which means that it is less likely to skid, which means that it is safer.' You, however, have considered that and have still come to the conclusion that the salesman is trying to sell you a fancy 'gizmo' that you do not really need or want.

Consider your thoughts if the salesman now points out to you the benefit of the car being safer, in other words, the ultimate benefit: 'This car has ABS brakes, which means that it is less likely to skid, which means that it is safer, which means that these brakes could actually save your life – or the lives of your family!' Now £100 sounds very reasonable in order to gain such a benefit (and how would you feel if you did not spend the apparent little extra?). The salesman only has to put a final reassurance in place to clinch the deal: 'I am sure that you are a safe driver and may not have considered having ABS brakes before, but you may wish to take this opportunity while you are changing your car to consider investing in them. After all, you know what the roads are like these days, and you may just be glad you decided to have them.' (Also note how the £100 extra cost for the brakes has now become an investment!)

It is the ultimate benefit that the customer seeks. Many businesses appear to be under the delusion that it is sufficient to simply 'lay out their stall'. Certainly customers need to know what is on offer, but 'laying out the stall' only ranks your offering alongside that of your competitors. Importantly in a pricing context, it also forces comparison between competing offerings to be made solely on the number of features that each competitor offers, rather than on the quality and usefulness of each feature. By just 'laying out your stall', a share of the available market may be gained, but that level of success is mediocre compared with what could be gained by taking the whole marketing process to the next level. It is poor marketing – and lazy selling – to leave it to the customer to figure out what the ultimate benefit is.

The ultimate benefit is reached quite simply: just keep saying 'which means that...' just as was done in the above example. All advertisements, all sales pitches, customer communications and actual service delivery should be delivering the same message: the ultimate benefit to the customer. 'Which means that...' should be the most spoken words and the most written or implied words in any visual medium used to communicate with customers. The example cited above used a tangible product, a car, to make this point. The identical process can be applied to any service situation: 'We have spent £x thousand pounds to upgrade our public service administrative facilities, which means that we can now offer you a much faster service, which means that you are not kept waiting around, which means less frustration for you and more time for you to do the things you really want to be doing.' Or, 'All of our corporate service staff are highly trained, which means that your needs will be dealt with promptly and efficiently, which means efficient cost-savings for your business because we aim to get things right first time.' Of course each of these examples is quite 'wordy' in order to convey the process of getting to the ultimate benefit and it might be better to distil the message down to the bare essentials, or 'sound-bite'.

The ultimate benefit for a public customer/consumer is invariably based on feelings and/or emotions. The ABS brakes example above appealed to feelings of security, and of 'having done the right thing'. The improvements in administrative facilities in the second example were used to convey the message that the customer can expect the transaction to be free of frustration, and holds the prospect of enjoyment for them by creating time for them to, 'do the things you would really like to be doing'. The cynics of the marketing world suggest that all consumer goods are sold on very basic yet powerful emotions such as fear, sex, greed, or guilt. Occasionally a sense of humour is used to promote goods also. Because of the intangibility and inseparability of services, and because of the intimate involvement of the customer within the service transaction, feelings and emotions are inevitably and inextricably bound up in the decisions customers make when choosing to purchase services, or when choosing between competing service providers.

In the corporate world, the prime motivations (ultimate benefits) for purchase decisions are: Will it save money? Will it make money? Will it transfer risk? This is not to say that emotions and feelings do not enter the equation, they do, but predominantly at the stage when a decision is to be made between otherwise more or less equal service providers, as perceived by the customer. 'No-one ever got fired for buying IBM' is a fairly well-known saying, implying that although IBM are rarely at the forefront of leading edge technology and are seldom the cheapest option available, their products are safe and their service reliable, that is you need not understand the technology, you need only agree the feelings of security arising from 'having made an overall sensible choice'.

Another way of looking at 'unique selling proposition' or 'competitive edge' is to apply the 'because...' test; the reason given by customers to justify their purchasing decision, in other words 'We always go to Bloggs & Co because...' Businesses providing services have to be particularly aware of the 'customer or consumer' issue raised in Chapter 2 and ensure that each party gains what they perceive as being the best ultimate benefit for them.

KEY POINTS

- People do not buy products or services – they buy the benefits they expect to gain from them.
- What your business offers can be described in terms of features, advantages and benefits. To be able to describe a feature in terms of benefits, simply keep saying, 'which means that…'
- The public tend to buy benefits offering positive feelings and/or emotions. Businesses first consider the financial aspects: Will it save money? Will it make money? Does it transfer risk?

ACTION POINTS

- List three main features your business offers to customers.
- Choose what you consider to be your strongest feature.
- Write 'which means that…' and state the advantage that feature conveys to the customer.
- Write 'which means that…' again to translate the advantage that feature into a benefit to the customer.
- Repeat this last step at least once more to get to an ultimate benefit that you should be marketing.
- What would your customers give as their reason for buying your service? What is your 'because…'? Whatever it is, it is the reason you are still in business.

PROBLEMS? WHAT PROBLEMS?

Sometimes a problem seems intractable, with no practical solution or no way of achieving the desired benefit. As an example of this, consider the problem posed to the owners of a particularly old skyscraper in New York. The various floors were let to different businesses, with some tenants renting several floors within the building. Staff of one of the tenant companies occupying several floors became frustrated over the slowness of the lifts and whenever they had the opportunity they asked other occupants of the lifts if they felt that the lifts were slow. People generally agreed and soon most people using the building were expressing feelings of frustration, and even anger, at how long it took them just to travel up and down from their offices. Complaints soon reached the building's owners, who became concerned that tenants might relocate to newer office blocks that had more efficient elevators.

A firm of engineers was duly commissioned to examine the problem and come up with a solution. After innumerable tests and inspections, the engineers reported that only a 3 per cent increase in lift speed was possible, allowing for the need to maintain safety and comfort for the passengers. The engineers did, however, suggest bolting brand new lifts onto the outside of the building. Of course, if this plan went ahead, it would be horrendously expensive and would cause major disruptions on every floor.

It appeared that the problem was insuperable, but then complaints from the original source started to die away and then stopped altogether. When the curious owners investigated, they found that the problem had been solved at a cost of only $50 a floor. The Personnel Director of the tenant company that had first complained of the slow lifts had simply installed a large mirror on the wall by the doors to each lift. The problem had been defined in terms of slowness of the lift, when the real problem appeared to have been the frustration caused by boredom experienced by people while waiting for the lift to arrive. The mirror gave people lots to look at – themselves and others – while having to wait with nothing else to do. Failure to interpret the problem correctly had led to solutions being sought from the wrong angle. The owners unceremoniously redecorated all the lobbies, installing mirrors by the side of the lift doors on every floor, and even in the lifts themselves, as part of the new interior design. There were no further complaints and the whole issue of slow lifts faded from memory.

Services are all about people. It is often useful to check the 'people issues' first to find possible solutions to otherwise apparently intractable problems.

The ultimate solution to a problem, however, may not be achievable. For example, solutions to public transport service problems range through trains, buses and taxis, aircraft and ferries. Each method has its own shortcomings and, to an extent, passengers exercise choice as to which one to suffer. They may prefer the speed of flight, yet have a fear of flying and thus choose the ferry. Or perhaps the train is quicker than a bus or coach, although the cost of the journey may be more expensive. Taking a taxi perhaps offers a more comfortable ride than a bus and requires little effort on the part of the passenger, yet may also be much more expensive than the bus. The ultimate solution in this scenario comprises four main factors: speed, safety, cost, effort. The ultimate solution might be to reach one's destination immediately, in absolute safety, at no cost and with no effort on one's own part. It is no wonder that *Star Trek*'s 'Beam me up, Scottie' seemed highly feasible and desirable in a science-fiction future!

The lesson for service providers is that, apart from issues of safety, customers may be prepared to trade off the remaining three factors against each other in order to gain maximum benefit for themselves. Passengers will be prepared to pay more if they need the journey to be quick, or more comfortable, with minimum effort on their part. They may be prepared to forego comfort for speed, or speed for comfort, but if a service provider can provide safe speed and comfort on a hassle-free journey, all at a reasonable cost, then passengers will not need to seek alternative solutions to their transport problems and the service providers' business should flourish.

No matter what you are selling, individuals buy because they have a problem and your product is seen as the solution to that problem. It may simultaneously solve other problems, but essentially a customer buys because something has triggered one main emotional or physical need. The problems that motivate organizations to buy are money-related. That is, your goods and/or services will help them to save money, make money, or to transfer risk.

KEY POINTS

- People seek solutions to problems caused by emotional or physical need. Goods and services are bought as ways of solving those problems. Organizations only buy to eventually save money, make money, or transfer risk.
- Only one problem is sufficient to trigger a purchase, although the purchase may simultaneously satisfy other needs in the customer.

- The customer would really like the 'ultimate solution', but recognizes that this is rarely obtainable by them. Trade-offs, therefore, take place to achieve the best balance of satisfaction.

ACTION POINTS

- Identify the main problem your customer needs to resolve.
- Identify the 'trigger' that causes the problem.
- Identify the 'ultimate solution' that your customers would really like, if it were possible. Are trade-offs being made by your customers, allowing room for a competitor to step in with a 'better' service offering?
- Decide which part of your service offering is most valued by your customer, and recognize what trade-offs you are forcing the customer to make.
- Take action to minimize the trade-off, or use it to illuminate the strength of your main benefit.

THE MARKETING MIX

The marketing mix is a term used to describe the combination of elements comprising the offer that a business makes to its customers. Many people are familiar with the four 'P's of the standard marketing mix for goods: Product, Place, Price and Promotion. These four elements fully describe the business offer for goods: What is the product? Where and how is it distributed and sold? What is the pricing policy? How is it promoted? If any one of these four elements is varied, then a new business offer is being made.

Because of the special characteristics of services, a further three 'P's are often added into the mix in order to fully describe the business offer. These are: physical evidence, people and process. Physical evidence is the tangibility of service facilities, and the physical outcome that may be derived from the service. In the case of a train service, for example, physical evidence relates to the presence of the train, its condition, the fact that it arrives at its destination, and the state of the passengers by the end of their journey. In the case of a business-to-business service, such as provision of staff training, physical evidence relates to quantifiable outcomes such as improved productivity, or less absenteeism, fewer accidents or quantifiable improvements in quality.

People are an integral part of providing a service, so changes in the numbers and/or types of staff involved and their levels of competence make significant differences to a service. If a bus is late, a waiting passenger's reaction and assessment of quality may be greatly affected by whether the driver apologizes and offers a valid reason, or whether the customer's wait is simply ignored. If a shop assistant appears indifferent to the customer, that customer's assessment of quality will be low and there may never be a repeat sale, irrespective of the quality of the goods on offer.

Process relates to how the service is actually provided and this includes the element of time. How do customers access the service? Processes that are in place solely for the service provider's benefit may become abused by customers and staff alike if they lead to delays and/or frustration for either of them. Do customers have to queue, or jump through any particular administrative hoops in order to benefit from the service? How is the service delivered? Are service staff directly involved, or is the process automated or self-service? If the process is automated, will the customer still class it as service? If there is no apparent gain in benefit to the customer, will it be viewed by the cynical customer as yet just one more example of cost-cutting, or that the company is distancing itself on purpose from customers that it does not really value as individuals? Some self-service supermarkets do not allow sufficient space for the shopper to pack their purchases after they have been checked through the till. The onus is blatantly put on to the customer to work like an employee in order to keep the queue moving!

The relevance of these seven 'P's to successful marketing is that any one of them can be used to provide a 'unique selling proposition'. Believing that customers are only interested in price ignores the other six factors in the overall business offer. This can result in poor financial returns that could have been greatly improved by marketing emphasis being placed on some of the other elements of the marketing mix. Analysing what the customer is buying, by ranking the business offer in terms of the customer's 'P' priority listing, can yield surprising results and may suggest changes in policies on how things are done, or how much is charged.

KEY POINTS

- Seven 'P's are often used to formulate the marketing mix for services: Product, Place, Price, Promotion, Physical evidence, People and Process.
- Any one of these can form the basis of a 'unique selling proposition'. A thoughtful combination of them can make a business unstoppable.
- Each of them deserves marketing attention.
- Selling only on Price is a poor option.

ACTION POINTS

- Find out the order in which your customer ranks the seven 'P's. (Price is rarely top.
- Align your business to what the customer wants.

COMPETITOR ANALYSIS AND FINDING THE GAP IN THE MARKET

Understanding the seven 'P's enables a service provider to make like-for-like comparisons between competitors' offerings and their own marketing mix. In this context, 'competitors' can be read as meaning either other companies similar to the service provider, for example, Smith versus Jones versus Bloggs, or alternative means by which the customer might achieve a similar end result, for example, rail travel might be compared against coach travel and against flying. Likewise, a named competitor might be compared against other competitors and against the service provider's own service.

Figure 3.1 shows a simple matrix with the seven 'P's in rows down the page and room for a number of competitors in columns across the page. The idea is that an objective description or rating is recorded in the relevant box for each competitor. Some boxes will inevitably have to contain your best subjective assessment, for example, 'good', 'fair', 'poor', 'high', 'low', etc, but the overall chart remains useful as long as identical criteria are used to assess each competitor – and your own business. The last column is for you to assess your own service business in the same way that you have assessed your competitors.

There are two ways to use this last column. First, you can record assessments of your current actual service and then compare the result against the assessments for your competitors. This will help you identify more closely who your real competitors are, and upon which fundamental points you are actually offering the same level of service and where your service is better than a competitor's. This knowledge makes for more effective advertising since you have identified a strong selling advantage/USP for that particular aspect of the marketing mix. Secondly, by studying the information you have recorded about the opposition, you can design your own service offering to be more competitive in certain key aspects, perhaps in a way that is new to the market. In other words, you can identify the gap in the market and, (assuming there is a market in the gap!), proceed to exploit it.

MIX	COMPETITOR 1	COMPETITOR 2	COMPETITOR 3	US
PRODUCT				
PLACE				
PRICE				
PROMOTION				
PHYSICAL EVIDENCE				
PEOPLE				
PROCESS				

Figure 3.1 *Assessment checklist*

WHAT MARKET ARE YOU REALLY IN?

It is at this point that it is necessary to identify exactly what market you are in. Just as the successful pub licensee knows that he or she is in the hospitality market – or even the entertainment market – rather than just retailing, so it is necessary to 'think outside the box' to identify clearly what your customer is actually buying. Is the insurance broker in insurance – or risk assessment? Is the banker in money – or customer care? Is the solicitor in law – or people's problems? Does the accountant only deal in numbers – or in what the numbers mean? Is the dentist in fillings – or smiles?

Knowing what market you are in helps you to tailor your advertising message to be aligned more closely with what your customer is really looking for. For example, the advertisement for a dentist's services might then read, 'Smile with confidence – Bloggs's caring dental services makes the difference!' The advertisement for an accountant taking work, and worry, from the shoulders of small business owners might read, 'Smiths Accountancy Services – for a less taxing business!'

If a business sells goods, the addition of an extra service element can readily differentiate it from its competitors and avoid reducing its prices. For example, if it sells fountain pens, is it in the pen market or the gift market? Reducing its prices rather defeats the objective for the customer who wants to spend their money on a gift of perceived value. Gift wrapping costs only the paper and ribbon, plus a few moments time for a trained member of staff, but the service would be seen as adding a significant amount of value for the customer by providing them with what they really wanted.

Identifying the right market becomes easier if the following question is asked: 'If my customer does not spend their money on these goods or services, what would they spend their money on instead?' Thus the competition to the fountain pen might not be a different make of pen, or a disposable ball-point, but a watch, a lighter, ear-rings or cuff-links. That is, what the customer is really seeking is not a pen, but any item of perceived value in a box.

For the service provider, it is vital to know what the customer wants in order to be able to establish a price. For example, if the customer just needs the benefit of someone who has a particular skill, or special tools or equipment, then almost any service provider in that field will suffice and price is a real competitive issue. If, however, the customer is seeking the known expert, 'the right person', then price takes second place. For example, the concert hall needing a violin player to make up the full complement of an orchestra will pay only the 'going rate' to obtain someone with the necessary skill. The price commanded by a famous soloist would be many times that figure. The pricing in some ladies' hairdressing salons often follows a similar pattern when a higher rate is charged for the personal skills of the proprietor.

Likewise, a firm needing technical consultancy input based upon a specific skill may negotiate hard to drive down the cost, or may similarly state that there is a 'going rate' that they will not breach. When the consultant's report is required to satisfy a worried external body, such as a firm's principal investors or government inspectors such as the Health and Safety Executive, the firm of consultants who are known to be expensive will be chosen, simply because they are well known and expensive. A particularly well-known firm of accountants may be chosen by a company to audit its accounts in order to reassure shareholders that the books have been properly audited, rather than to achieve any quality improvement in the actual preparation of the accounts beyond that which any competent firm of accountants could have produced at lower cost.

To an extent, the market a business is in revolves around whether its goods or services are *needed* or *wanted*. The customer may need a pen, or want to buy a nice gift. The need for a pen is satisfied by the inexpensive disposable ball-point, the desire for a suitable gift is satisfied at a much higher price. Goods and services purchased out of need will be far more price-sensitive than those bought because they are wanted. Drivers needing repairs to their family car will seek and consider prices quoted from various mechanics, whereas the owner of a classic sports car kept for special occasions may want to have it repaired and cared for by 'the expert' and will be prepared to pay a much higher charge. An implication of this may be that the classic sports car repairer only needs to work on a few cars in order to recover the overheads of the business, whereas the general mechanic has to do a much higher volume of work to achieve recovery of overheads. Such pricing issues and many more factors affecting price are dealt with in detail in Chapter 5: Pricing for profit.

KEY POINTS

- The successful business identifies clearly what market(s) it is in.
- By doing so it can more readily identify its real competitors: 'If your potential customers are not spending their money on your service, what are they spending it on?'
- The successful business then proceeds to align itself to the market and appeal to the market through the message it gives in its advertisements and all customer communications.
- Pricing of services is a function of needs versus wants, and 'just the skill' versus 'the right person'.

ACTION POINTS

- Identify what market you are in.
- Use that knowledge to clearly identify your real competitors.
- Re-appraise your advertising message and mission statement.
- Identify whether your service is 'needed' or 'wanted'. Adjust your service offering and/or pricing accordingly.
- Be the expert, not the generalist.

BRANDING

Branding is all about managing customers' expectations and consistency. Because of the special characteristics of services (see Chapter 2), people can be particularly wary of making the right choice of service provider. Many branded goods are available from many shops, but which shops do customers frequent most often in order to buy them? For customers, knowing in advance the quality of service that might be expected makes all the difference as to which service provider is patronized by them. Branding adds confidence to the purchase. In effect it states a promise, and an awareness on the part of the supplier that they have something worth losing – the reputation associated with the brand name.

Branding is often used to promote a service since it can be difficult trying to otherwise encapsulate the intangibility, emotions or other outcomes of a service. The advertising message is thus often conveyed by a mission statement perhaps accompanied by carefully worded descriptions or pictures of the facilities available and/or pictures of 'happy, smiling customers' who are using the facilities or have just used them. Logos, trade marks, emblems and distinctive colours are all used to convey the image and tone of the service provider and differentiate it from others, particularly in a crowded business environment such as a shopping centre, a directory that is full of competing advertisers, or on the Web.

Because branding relies on consistency and yet a characteristic of services is that they are variable, many branded service providers regularize their set procedures by the use of operating manuals or dedicated screen software to guide staff through the process in a highly controlled fashion. 'Mystery shoppers' are often used to police the system so that centralized management can obtain relatively objective reports on whether the prescribed system is actually being delivered and where, how and when it is not. Standardization of forms, equipment, facilities, ingredients, methods, policies and procedures all combine to remove variability from the service in an effort to achieve consistency of standards. For example, the replication of a proven process is the basis of all branded business format franchises and can be highly successful. In this scenario, the service provider need not necessarily be an accomplished expert in their field but simply trained to deliver the prescribed business format. A strength of business format franchising is that it can combine the proven systems and resources of a large franchisor together with the motivation and local knowledge of the investing franchisee to provide a high level of service to the customer.

A systemized approach can be efficient for most transactions, although there can inevitably be occasions when a customer's special wishes can not be accommodated by the system. In this event, the service is assessed by the customer as being poor because the system is inflexible and thus impersonal. In a franchised business, a franchisee might also consider the business format or system too inflexible if their own wish is to quickly respond to trends by adding to, or changing, the products. Mechanisms are often in place to allow, or indeed encourage, 'best practice' discussions, but improvements have to be adopted by the franchisor and the entire franchise network if the integrity and consistency of the franchise brand is to be protected.

Perhaps demand for the service is such that strict systems must be adhered to in order for target customers to be dealt with quickly and efficiently. However, many staff in a service environment like to be able to inject their own flair and ideas into the business, particularly when dealing directly with customers. Will these staff become demoralized or demotivated by the apparent de-skilling of their jobs brought about by regularizing or standardizing procedures? Would investment in better recruitment and training of staff to deal in all situations be better than investment in systems that limit their initiative?

KEY POINTS

- Branding is to do with managing customer expectations consistently. It adds confidence by reducing the risk of bad service.
- Branding is used to convey the essence of what the service is about and may be represented through a brand name, logo, emblem, trade mark or specific colours. The use of such devices is particularly important in an environment or medium containing many competing advertisers.
- Branding may require the process to be regimented in order to reduce variation. Methods and procedures may be strictly controlled according to a prescribed system. These may be too rigid for some customers (and possibly some employees!).
- Branded services lend themselves to business format franchising, which generally rely upon a specifically trained local franchisee who is committed to following the procedures set by the franchisor.

ACTION POINTS

- Decide how your service might be better branded.
- Regularize consistent service delivery wherever possible if you wish to reduce variability, but be aware that set procedures might make your business appear too rigid for some customers and/or your staff.
- Write a clear and concise mission statement to tell your customers (and employees, suppliers, shareholders, the media, etc) what it is that you provide.

● If you cannot sum up your entire business offering in a mission statement comprising only one or two sentences, how do you expect your
potential customers (and staff) to understand, in essence, what it is that
you do and what your concerns are?

THE AUGMENTED PRODUCT AND ADDED-VALUE

With thousands of outlets in hundreds of countries, the
McDonald's franchise is widely recognized as perhaps the most
successful retail catering operation on the planet. On that fact
alone it would be reasonable to say that their burgers must be the
best in the world. Whilst some people may insist that they are,
there are many, including some of McDonald's existing customers,
who would disagree. It is, however, a good example of, 'Ask not
what you are selling, but what is the customer buying?' You might
expect McDonald's to say that they sell burgers, yet if you asked a
customer in McDonald's why they were there, they might reply
that it's convenient, or quick, or all they have time for, that the staff
are friendly or efficient, the facilities are clean and hygienic, it's air-
conditioned, or there's ample car parking. They might point out
that the location is handy, the price is fair, or that at least you know
what you are going to get every time you visit. They may just say
that their kids or grandchildren dragged them in! The irony is that
very few customers actually mention the product – the burger!
McDonald's are a good example of what marketing people call the
'augmented product', that is, the actual product is surrounded by
additional goods or services that altogether make up a package of
customer expectations.

An analogy can be drawn between McDonald's and, say,
professional consulting. If you ask the customers of a particular
consulting firm why they chose that firm, the answer may be
that the firm is professional, reliable or trustworthy and can
maintain confidences; or that they are punctual, or pleasant to
work with, offer specialist facilities; or can be very flexible, etc.
It is these factors that are the selling points for most professional
service providers such as consultants, financial advisers, accountants, solicitors, lawyers, insurance brokers, doctors, trainers,
tutors, designers, etc. The actual quality of the consultancy,

recommendations, reports or other outcomes cannot be commented upon until after they have been produced – after involvement in the service is close to completion. Of course, experience of the quality of these items is a factor considered by the customer in a repeat or on-going relationship.

Adding value to goods or services by providing extra service is at the heart of improving profits without cutting costs. As was seen earlier in this chapter, in the example of providing a gift-wrapping, a customer might perceive greater benefit by patronizing the supplier who added the value of the gift-wrap compared against the lack of such extra benefit from one who did not. When all other aspects are equal, the extra facility of room service, or emergency overnight laundry, etc, at an hotel can influence a potential customer's decision as to which hotel to choose. A small premium may then be seen to be reasonable. We are used to the concept of paying extra for fast developing of photographs, same-day delivery service for goods, delivery of daily newspapers and milk, a comfortable lounge at an airport, and prompt personal attention from professionals.

As a variation on this theme, consider the example of an odd-job man whom we shall call George. George had taken early retirement at age 50, on a pension that was barely adequate. He needed to supplement his income in some way and decided that he would prefer to be self-employed, so that he could choose his own work and, to some extent, his working times. George had always been relatively fit and did not feel 50 years of age! He wanted an active occupation that would not be too strenuous and he enjoyed working outdoors whenever possible. George was a 'people person' and, having done some research into possible local demand for 'handyman' services, decided to offer his services to householders, including senior citizens, in the local neighbourhood.

George soon found that whilst there was certainly demand for a handyman, none of the jobs that people asked him to quote for was really worth the money he needed to charge to cover his time, travel and effort. George changed his strategy. He realized that what people were buying was his time, so he had to make his time cost-effective and worthwhile for the customer. Now, if someone asked him to mow their lawn, which might take only an hour, George would look at the garden and suggest that when he came to mow the lawn he could perhaps also mend their broken gate, collect up all the leaves from the garden and change the washer on a leaking tap in their kitchen. That would be a morning's work, for which he felt he could charge the price he needed. The customer was delighted at the prospect of getting so many different things done in one go; the job was cost-effective for both parties, and very soon George had all the half days and full days of jobs that he could want.

KEY POINTS

- Goods and services can be augmented by ancillary factors, which may be seen in many respects as being more important than the core product. ('What is the customer buying?').This is particularly relevant when a customer is choosing a service provider for the first time.
- Added value arises when a facility or service (at relatively little cost to the provider) is added to the core item or service to improve the level of perceived benefit of the whole to the customer. This can act as a unique selling proposition and may either allow a small premium to be charged, yielding a much higher percentage profit overall, or create a new 'package' that is attractive to the customer and at the (higher) price needed to charge to make the job worthwhile.

ACTION POINTS

- In the centre of a sheet of paper, write down the core 'product' that you sell. Draw eight spokes radiating from the centre. Between each of the spokes write down what else a customer is getting when they buy from you, (eg promptness, reliability, trustworthiness, friendly service, professionalism, no-quibble warranty, etc).
- Could any of these descriptions, or the total as a whole, be used as unique selling points or as a reason for charging a small premium?
- Identify other services that you might add to your existing offering to improve perceived value of benefit to the customer.

SEGMENTATION

It is a rather obvious statement of fact that not all customers are identical. Even if they appear to want the same service, there will be major variations in how, when, where, why, and from whom a service will be preferred. The price that different customers are prepared to pay will also be a function of how closely the service meets their individual needs. To enable a business to rationalize its offering and maximize its profit, customers who share similar characteristics can be grouped together to form market segments for marketing purposes. One single homogenous characteristic is all that is needed to create a segment, such as all males in one segment, or all females in another; alternatively all sole traders in one segment, all partnerships in another, all limited companies make up a third segment, and perhaps all Plcs in a fourth. As more homogenous characteristics are overlaid, quite specific types of customer can be identified. For example, all vegetarian restaurants in London run by sole-traders who require specialist delivery services in refrigerated vehicles to their premises early each morning.

Often referred to as niche marketing, appealing to a specific type of customer can be highly profitable. Strategically, the service provider whose business involves selling or providing goods of some sort is purposely not selling just on volume. Stocks can be therefore lower than when aiming purely for volume sales and this can not only ease potential cash flow problems but also yield a higher return on capital employed. Fewer, yet higher value, sales allow the supplier to deliver on a promise of good service, retaining customer loyalty and a more predictable level of business for the medium and longer term. (See Chapter 5: Pricing for profit.) Because customers are normally involved in the service process, and there is no long supply chain, service providers are usually much closer to their customers/consumers than manufacturers of goods are to theirs. One reason for large amounts of money being spent on the media advertising of consumer goods is that manufacturers do not know who their customers are. It is certainly obvious that manufacturers spend further large amounts of money on market research trying to find out. Service providers on the other hand may well know a great deal about all of their individual customers. As will be seen later, this knowledge can play a key role in determining optimum marketing strategies, particularly in respect of decisions relating to pricing policies, advertising and promotional activity, and strategic business development. For the service provider, segmentation of existing customers can often be based upon market intelligence that is either readily available within the company, or is within relatively easy reach of it.

Different market sectors may exist, each perhaps requiring very different approaches by the service provider. Each sector may be re-classified into component segments representing homogenous groupings of potential customers. Sectors basically represent the environment in which the service is provided, and the major customer groupings, often differentiated by their origins or industry. Notably, the public sector often has differing requirements to the industrial and commercial sectors and each may be regulated by different laws and systems of control. Within the industrial sector, reference might likewise be made to the automotive sector, or pharmaceutical industry, the media, or education sector, etc.

The purpose of segmentation is to aid the marketing process, making it more accurate and thus more efficient, productive and profitable. The service provider should be able to tailor the provision of the service to the customer so that it is perceived as being the right level of service, provided in the right place, at the right time, by the right methods and delivered by the right people. The customer will then expect to pay the right price for the service they want. Importantly, segmentation enables the service provider to target the right type of customer; one that appreciates the service, will pay the right price and will use the service again. Just advertising by a scatter-gun approach inevitably also attracts the 'customer from hell!' Identifying the right customer is a secret of success for many firms and segmentation helps to clarify such identification. Management attention can be focused on an effective mission statement and the strategies needed for achieving its stated objectives.

As an example of how segmentation can help a service business, consider the case of a small printing business offering a variety of design and print services, run by a sole-trader whom we shall name Kate. Kate has identified the following markets for her services:

Local small/medium sized businesses

Design and printing of business stationery, promotional leaflets, etc
Christmas cards and calendars

Large companies within a 30 mile radius

Volume printing of business stationery
Christmas cards and calendars
Promotional literature
Diaries

Charities and other organizations

Christmas cards and calendars
Raffle tickets, etc

General public

Christmas cards
Wedding and personal stationery

Each one of these groups can be defined as a target market segment. By producing a matrix of product versus customer, Kate can clearly identify what she is supplying to whom. The matrix is shown in Figure 3.2.

This matrix can now be used in many different ways to aid Kate's marketing strategies, since different pricing policies and promotional activities may need to be implemented for each target market segment. These issues will be covered in depth in each of the relevant later chapters.

	Small/medium businesses	Large companies	Charities, etc	General Public
Design	+	–	–	–
Business stationery	+	+	–	–
Promotional leaflets	+	+	–	–
Christmas cards, etc	+	+	+	+
Raffle tickets, etc	–	–	+	–
Personal stationery	–	–	–	+

Figure 3.2 *Product/customer matrix*

KEY POINTS

● Segmentation is the process of classifying customers, and potential customers, into homogenous groups, that is types of customer who share similar characteristics. Such characteristics for the public might be age, socio-economic circumstance, geographic/demographic location, purpose for wanting the service, etc. For businesses, these might be corporate size, industrial sector, geographic location, purpose for wanting the service, etc.

● Segmentation enables better margins to be obtained and more efficient business, perhaps through reducing capital expenditure required, or improving cash flow through lower stock-holding needs for those service providers whose business involves transfer of ownership of goods.

● Customer loyalty can be enhanced by providing services tailored to customer needs.

● Segmentation concentrates management attention on the customer and identifies other possible areas of opportunity.

Segment your market

ACTION POINTS

- Identify who your customers are. This information is usually more accessible for service providers than it is for manufacturers as there is not normally a chain of intermediaries between the service provider and the customer/consumer.
- Note any defining characteristics that can be applied to group them into coherent market segments.
- Define the market segments you currently serve.
- Define market segments that might provide further business opportunities.

SEGMENTATION, TARGETING AND POSITIONING

Segmentation is the first stage of a three-part process designed to help market a service for profit. Having identified customers into coherent groups, the second stage in the process is to target each group. That is, to aim the service and all related advertising and promotional activity exclusively at that group. The third stage of the marketing process is to position the service to be attractive to the chosen target market segment. The terms of the service, and what the advertising actually says, will be totally dependent upon the needs and wants of the specific group.

This process is akin to going fishing. The first part of the process is to decide exactly what you want from your day's fishing: why you are doing it. (This fact may seem obvious, but it is surprising how many businesses start 'fishing' without having clearly decided exactly what their mission is and what quantifiable results they want from their efforts). You then decide what type of fish you are setting out to catch (segmentation), as this significantly improves your chances of success since you will tailor your efforts to catching that particular type of fish. You do some research to find out whether there are perhaps more fish this year than last year, that is what the trend is and whether your plans are fundamentally viable. For businesses, this is what 'understanding your market' is all about.

As further research to improve your chance of success, you find out as much as you can about the normal habits of the type of fish you want to catch. You will then 'target' that type of fish, by finding out where the best place might be to catch them, when would be the best time of year, even perhaps the best time of day, how they feed and on what do they feed, etc. All this information then enables you to 'position' your efforts to be attractive to that type of fish. For trout, you may fish in a fast-running river using a fly as a lure, simply because trout often like to catch insects that land on the water's surface. To catch a mackerel, however, you would be sea-fishing and perhaps using a mackerel spinner – something that looks like a small fish swimming well below the water's surface. Whether you are catching trout or mackerel, you are still an angler. For businesses, this is what 'understanding your customer' is all about.

Successful marketing is all about correct 'positioning', offering each type of customer what they want and in a way that they prefer. For example, how seat reservations are sold for flights on Concorde depends a great deal on whether the target customers are business people looking for a fast, comfortable journey to a distant destination, or whether they are day-trippers just wanting to enjoy the experience of a short flight on Concorde. Customer expectations in each case will be very different and the service, pricing, and all other aspects are tailored to suit their needs. Tickets for a day-trip on Concorde are even sold as gifts for people, or offered as prizes in promotions for other businesses. Thus Concorde, like many other services, can earn profit for the service provider by operating in many different markets, as a result of segmentation, targeting and positioning.

Positioning correctly means clearly defining each of the seven 'P's that make up the marketing mix and using variations of the mix to satisfy each target segment of the overall market. That is, deciding exactly what that type of customer wants as the 'product'; how and where they prefer to buy it; how much they are prepared to pay for it; how best to promote the service to them; what physical evidence the customer will expect as proof of good service; what type of person they prefer to deliver the service; and exactly how they prefer the service to be provided.

Position yourself to be attractive to your customer...

KEY POINTS

- The three stages in the process of successful service marketing are: segmentation, targeting and positioning.
- Targeting is the process of finding out everything you can about the chosen market segment and the customers who comprise it, and then using that knowledge to aim the business offer.
- Positioning is the process of making the service offer attractive to a particular target market segment or to very different markets, by varying one or more of the seven 'P's of the marketing mix.

ACTION POINTS

- Decide which target market segments you want to aim at.
- Prioritize the order in which you want to tackle them.
- Thoroughly research your first chosen target market segment: identify the trends in the market and everything there is to know about the buying habits and wants of the customers that make up the segment. (See Chapter 4: Strategic direction decisions.)
- List the seven 'P's of the marketing mix and write next to each of them exactly how that part of the mix is to be best provided, that is, your formula for success in selling profitably to that target market segment.
- Repeat the process for each chosen target market segment.
- Rearrange your priority list of target market segments in light of the research information you have gleaned and a realistic assessment of your firm's capabilities.
- If necessary, realign your current service offering to more closely match the needs of your current target market segments, and plan your campaign for tackling any target market segment you have chosen that is new to you.

4

Strategic direction decisions

' "Which way do I go from here?" asked Alice to the Cheshire Cat. "That depends a great deal on where you want to get to," replied the Cat.' (Lewis Carroll: *Alice in Wonderland*).

The previous chapter culminated with the marketing concepts and techniques of segmentation, targeting and positioning. This chapter is all about being in the right markets and targeting the right types of customer within those markets. In these respects it is to do with gathering, analysing and using knowledge gained from market research, market intelligence and customer feedback. The process is that of trying to gain the wisdom that comes with experience, without the possible repercussions of having to live through unwanted business catastrophes.

Business advisers are often heard to say to their clients: 'You must research your market' or 'You must understand your market' and/or 'You must understand your customer'. Yet advice is seldom offered on exactly how such research should be conducted and how such understanding can be achieved. This chapter attempts to describe the processes that will enable you to gather information on which you can act to position your service to be attractive to your target customer. As described in an earlier chapter: if you do not have a customer, you do not have a business.

To this we can now add: if you do not have the right customer, you do not have the right business.

It is easy to selectively manipulate statistics or other research 'findings' to prove that anything is either possible or impossible. The truth may be brilliantly illuminated, or somewhere within shades of grey. Either way, it is of course essential to view all research findings dispassionately and with absolute objectivity.

THE TRUTH IS OUT THERE

Understanding your market(s) is key to maximizing opportunity and surviving the competition. The service provider's own view of the market and the knowledge gained from operating in it, perhaps for many years, is of course invaluable and a real asset to the business. It can be maximized by installing systems that gather the necessary market intelligence and on-going data as a matter of

routine, in the same way as financial data is collected and recorded to ensure control of the business. Analysis of such data can be fed back to operations so that market trends are tracked and management can execute optimal strategies for the short, medium and long term success of the business. It is, however, only one perspective, and it can be deceiving.

Conventional wisdom can sometimes prevail over common sense so that we remain blind to an obvious truth. For example, for centuries Europeans believed that the earth was flat. This was despite the evidence of their own eyes when watching a sailing ship sail over the horizon towards them, when at first just the mast is seen and only later does the whole boat come into view. If the earth were flat, then the whole boat would be seen at once, albeit as a small dot on the horizon but the whole growing larger as it drew closer. Likewise, it was believed that the sun revolved around the earth although, in this case, it was because that was what was seen by people every day.

Having input from at least a second perspective can thus be valuable in establishing the truth – Galileo's life would have been much easier if he had had satellite photographs of the earth! The truth is indeed 'out there'. Having three points of reference would undoubtedly validate information, just as modern navigation is very much aided by satellite positioning systems that rely upon a trigonometry of beacons, so business knowledge can be verified by considering three views on the same market. As discussed above, the service provider's own perspective is invaluable, but that knowledge can be supplemented by perspectives from two further vantage points: from the view of the industry, and the customer's viewpoint.

The industry's view is used here as a collective term to describe all the information available from anyone else with an interest in the market. It will thus include: published reports; surveys; seminars; and media commentary such as in published articles, journals, business magazines, newspapers, on television or on the Internet. The performance of competitors, their activities and comments, and their advertising and promotional campaigns all add to an overall view of trends in the marketplace, as does information gleaned from exhibitions, trade fairs, and shows. Suppliers have a vested interest in understanding the market in order to be able to anticipate the needs of the service provider and be ready to supply to them. The views of professional bodies, trade associations, and the opinions of colleagues in ancillary or associated markets are all worth counselling, particularly in respect of potential opportunities or threats that the market might face in the future.

Listening to the views of customers in the chosen target market segment is absolutely critical for success. Understanding their view of the market and hearing what they really want, perhaps also finding out what they would really like (the 'ultimate benefit' and the 'ultimate solution' as described in Chapter 3), are possibly the most fruitful research activities a service provider can undertake. Finding out where potential customers currently go for the service that you can provide identifies your real competitors, and these may not be the ones you thought you were up against. Finding out why the competitor's service is chosen in preference to your own – not guessing why – can sometimes yield surprising home-truths. A business can sometimes learn useful lessons from its competitors and identifying the competitors' unique selling points, as perceived by the customer, enables a business to combat them through its own strategies (see Chapter 3, Figure 3.1).

You may find that your customers are also your competitor's customers, that services offered by both of you are used by customers at different times or to satisfy different needs. It is not unknown for customers to use what they perceive is the best (or perhaps the only) option available for them in each category of 'product' or service, having little sense of loyalty towards one particular service provider for all of their needs. For an example, one only has to think of the domestic insurance services industry for clear illustration of this point. In any household, house contents might be insured through a broker who has recommended a policy type from one particular firm, whereas buildings insurance may have been arranged through a building society acting for a totally different insurance company. Holiday insurance might be arranged through a travel agent acting also as agent for yet another insurer, medical insurance might be supplied by an employer, pet insurance can be arranged with yet another firm through the vet, and the car might be insured by a policy bought directly by the customer over the telephone!

In the above example, the customer may not think of asking the broker who arranged a house contents insurance about buildings

Listen to the customer

insurance for the house, holiday insurance, or insurance to cover veterinary surgery bills for their pets. The broker may simply not be perceived as being in these markets at all! A trend in the market may be that, as the householder gets used to buying car insurance by telephone, then each of the other types of insurance will come to be bought over the phone and the telephone replaces the broker as the (self-)service provider for all domestic insurance.

KEY POINTS

● Understanding your market is crucial for success. Analysis of trends can yield surprising results. Market research in this context is largely to do with estimating the numbers of potential customers and hence the fundamental viability of the business.

- There are three possible viewpoints, each of which should be explored rigorously: your own objective knowledge and experience of market trends; the views and opinions of the industry; and the views and opinions of customers and potential customers. What do customers really want?
- Finding out who your real competitors are, and what their actual unique selling points are or how they manage to get their customers, can help in determining your own marketing strategies.
- Customers may be quite discerning, yet on other occasions apparently quite indiscriminate about selecting what is on offer from different service providers at different times or to satisfy different wants or needs. The more you know about customer behaviour, the more you can help your business.

ACTION POINTS

- Divide a sheet of paper into three columns: In the first column, list everything you know about the trends in your chosen target market.
- Gather as much up-to-date information about your chosen target market as possible from 'the industry'.
- In the second column of your sheet of paper, list the results of up-to-date research information about market trends gathered from 'the industry'. Does this information reinforce your understanding of the market as listed in the first column, or does some of this fresh information appear to conflict with your own views?
- Use the third column to list results of live research about 'the market' carried out with customers and potential customers. Record whose services they use, and on what occasions, and for what reasons. Find out why they do not use your service. Find out how they perceive the market. In what 'categories' do they put different products and services. What they include in any particular market may not coincide with your categorizations and their view of the market may not include you in it at all!
- Consider all the information you have gathered and use it to determine your optimum strategy within that chosen target market segment.

YOU ARE NOT YOUR CUSTOMER

A simple yet perceptive observation, often overlooked by many salespeople, is that they are not their own customer. That they are the only people in the world they are not selling to. It is the customer's preferences, needs, wants, and definition of quality that should prevail in the transaction. It is very easy to slip into trying to sell the type of service we would like, into assuming that it is what the customer wants. Of course, there is general consensus as to what makes up good service: reliability, efficiency, promptness, friendliness, politeness, etc. But what we do not know is the order of priority that the customer places on these virtues. For example, a passenger ferry might concentrate its effort on providing a comfortable journey, when some passengers are more concerned with getting to their destination quickly. Passengers taking their car across the English Channel en route to southern France might be eager to get on with their journey. On the other hand, some passengers may prefer a leisurely, comfortable crossing. Those same car drivers returning from southern France might choose a comfortable ferry crossing back to England because it provides them with time to rest after a long drive, before the final leg home.

Having a policy of regularly asking customers' opinions, listening and taking heed of their answers allows the service provider to align the service with the same order of priority as the customer wants. That service provider will, as a result, be seen as 'the natural choice' for customers in that target market segment. An implication is that, as only one aspect of the marketing mix, pricing can also be a matter of preference. Customers will quickly let you know if they think you are genuinely overcharging for your service and competitors provide an indication of 'the going rate'. Undercharging is often the result of the service provider considering only his or her own views about money. The fair price is what the customer considers to be fair, considering the quality of the service.

A great deal of probing has to be carried out, with the positive assistance of the customer, if the service is to truly satisfy their needs. Understanding the customer is all about learning the answers to the following 'open' questions (questions that do not invite a simple yes/no answer):

- Who is the buyer? Who is the customer, and who is the consumer? (See Chapter 2.)
- What sort of person is the customer? What are the characteristics of your chosen target market segment?
- What do they want? What would they really like? (What would they value?)
- How do they want it? By what means would they prefer to pay for it? How often do they prefer or need to buy?
- Why are they buying it? (See Chapter 3: Features, advantages, benefits – and the ultimate benefit.)
- When do they buy? Is there a seasonality to sales? When in their life do they buy?
- Where do they buy? Where would they prefer to buy? How do they prefer to buy?

Each of the above questions is self-explanatory, but one of the questions merits further consideration: When do they buy? This question indicates that there is usually a 'trigger' that initiates the customer's interest in the service.

Understanding this trigger can be the key to successful advertising, since advertising money spent at this point will more likely be heeded by a receptive customer. Finding out what the trigger is for different types of customer enables a service provider to better anticipate demand and be in a position to plan for it. The trigger may be obvious, such as the end of the school term in July for the start of the main holiday season for families; or it might be a little more obscure, such as a rise in land or property values might prompt people to decide that they really should have a will written. Just as the experienced angler knows when to expect a good catch, so the demand for a service can peak at certain times. Demand for many services can be cyclical, rising and falling according to the season of the year, the weather, or longer term factors such as the numbers of people reaching a certain age group. The need for driving instructor services is fuelled by the numbers of young people reaching age 17, and demand for financial services increases as more people take early retirement or voluntary severance packages from employment.

Often the trigger is beyond control of the service provider, but it can be perhaps anticipated as it often arises from changes in customers' circumstances or in the environment in which they exist. Awareness of social, legal, economic, and political trends affecting customers can be invaluable in determining when the customer might be receptive to the marketing message. Advances in technology can bring services within reach of a wider or different customer base, offering new and different opportunities for the service provider. Likewise, changes in the above factors can pose threats to an existing service provision.

KEY POINTS

- You are not your customer.
- Your preferences are to a great extent irrelevant. What matters is: what does the customer want?
- A service business will be more successful if it aligns its order of priorities to match those of its customers.
- Undercharging can be avoided by pricing according to the customer's view of what is a fair price.
- Understanding of your customer arises from asking them lots of 'open' questions: Who? What? Where? How? When? and Why? And then listening to, and heeding, their answers. Aligning your service offer to fit their answers makes your service the natural choice for those target customers.
- Possible opportunities (and threats) for your business can be identified from an understanding of current and expected future changes to social, legal, economic, political and technological factors surrounding your target customer.
- Potential customers may know about your service, but there is usually a trigger that makes them act on that knowledge and seek the sort of service you are offering. When do they buy?
- The trigger may appear to be obvious, but there may also be more obscure or subtle reasons that trigger the customer's need for the service.
- Identifying the triggers and using that knowledge helps you deliver a timely and pertinent advertising message to receptive potential customers.

ACTION POINTS

- Install systems into your service provision to ensure that customers preferences are identified and heeded.
- Plan and implement a policy of collecting and collating information arising from customers' answers to the open questions described above.
- Re-examine your pricing policies, to ensure they are aligned to what the customer considers to be a fair price.
- Undertake assessments of possible opportunities and threats arising from changes in the social, legal, economic, and political environment and identify how technological advances will affect your customers.
- Identify the triggers that make your potential customers receptive to your advertising message. Align your marketing plans accordingly.

Having looked at service aspects to do with the customer, strategies for identifying target market segments, and mechanisms for researching them, the next stage is to decide whether servicing a chosen target market segment is viable for your business, and to plan your business development strategies. The following section considers some of the factors affecting choice of direction for a service provider.

As with the management of any project, the first question is: What exactly are we trying to achieve? The second question is: When do we need to achieve it by? And finally: What resources of time, money, people, facilities, equipment, etc do we need to accomplish the plan? Deciding the right direction for the business depends upon where you see the business as being in, say, three years' time. What is your vision for the medium and long term future? What should be the overall mission of the business, and to whom should responsibility for its success be entrusted? To start the planning process, it is first necessary to identify the viability (or otherwise) of chosen target market segments.

BREAK-EVEN

Having researched a possible target market, the service provider needs to know the minimum level of business required to make entry into the market feasible. The break-even point is the point at which the business has just covered all of its costs but is not yet showing a profit. This 'critical mass' can be described in terms of the minimum number of customers needed to cover all overheads (fixed costs) and any variable costs associated with providing the service to those customers. A calculation of customer numbers required for break-even relies upon the price, or prices, charged for the service. Alternatively, break-even can be described in financial terms, that is the level of turnover (sales) needed to cover both fixed and variable costs.

The number of customers required to achieve break-even can be compared with the forecast of potential customer numbers that arises from market research, assuming 'fair prices' are to be charged. A calculation can be made of market share needed to achieve an adequate profit. The service provider then needs to assess their organization's ability to meet and exceed the break-even volume of customers needed to make the business viable for them. Constraints of time, physical resources, or staff capability may mean that a particular market segment is not to be feasible for that service provider.

The ability to calculate break-even relies upon knowing the financial costs involved in delivering the service. Each element of cost can be classified as being either fixed cost (overhead), or variable cost. Fixed costs include all those costs that do not vary directly with the number of customers; such costs would include salaries, insurances, rent, rates, heat, light and power, vehicles, etc. Variable costs include any cost incurred directly as a result of serving customers and are, therefore, those elements of cost that go up or down, dependent only upon the number of customers served. For example, fixed costs for a restaurant might include the chef's salary or wage, whereas the cost of food provided to customers is variable since it depends upon how many customers there are (and their choices from the menu).

To be able to calculate break-even, one first needs to produce the Trading and Profit & Loss (P&L) figures. The standard way of calculating profit (or loss) is to start with the figure for sales and from this deduct the total of the variable costs. This calculation gives rise to the figure of Gross Profit. If the Gross Profit is then divided by the sales figure, and the answer is multiplied by 100, this identifies the level of Gross Profit Margin achieved expressed as a percentage of sales. Break-even will be inversely proportional to the Gross Profit Margin (GPM); that is, break-even will go down if the GPM goes up. In other words, the better the GPM, the lower the sales level needed to break-even; and the lower the GPM, the higher the sales level needed.

Having calculated the Gross Profit, the figure for fixed costs (overheads) has to be deducted in order to arrive at the Net Profit (or Loss). It is apparent that break-even will be directly proportional to the amount of fixed costs; if the cost of, say, insurance rises, then break-even also goes up. If savings can be made by reducing overheads, then the level of sales needed to break-even will fall. It can, therefore, be said that break-even is directly proportional to overheads and inversely proportional to Gross Profit Margin. These relationships can be converted to a simple mathematical equation:

$$\text{Break-even} = \frac{\text{£ Overheads} \times 100}{\text{Gross Profit Margin \%}}$$

The number of customers needed to achieve break-even is obtained by dividing the break-even sales figure by the price charged to each customer. Of course, the higher the price, the fewer the customers needed to achieve break-even. Pricing is thus a consequence of positioning: making the service offer attractive to a small number of high paying customers, or larger numbers of customers who are in the lower or mid-price market segment.

If the break-even calculation calls for a higher price to be charged than was originally envisaged, the service offer or quality might be improved at little cost to the service provider in order to command the increased price needed to make the whole plan viable (see Chapter 3: The augmented product and added-value). Once break-even has been achieved then profit is earned as the amount remaining from sales after consequent variable costs have been deducted.

For those service providers such as consultants or other professionals who incur only nominal variable costs, break-even is mostly determined by the cost of their business overheads, since their GPM is nearly 100 per cent. To find the 'break-even' that achieves any particular level of profit you require, simply add that amount as an extra overhead in the equation.

KEY POINTS

- To be able to make strategic direction decisions, you need to first set the objectives for your business. (If there are no goal posts, how do you know when you have scored?)
- Break-even is the level of sales needed to cover all costs, both fixed and variable, before a profit starts to be earned. Profit then accumulates at the rate of increase in sales minus the variable costs incurred in making those extra sales.
- Gross Profit is the amount of money remaining after variable costs have been deducted from the sales figure. Gross Profit Margin is the Gross Profit expressed as a percentage of the sales figure.
- Break-even equals fixed costs times 100, divided by the Gross Profit Margin.
- Calculating break-even will help to identify the viability of a proposed service, since the break-even sales figure required can be compared against market research predictions of numbers of possible customers and the sort of prices they might be prepared to pay. (Not only 'is there a gap in the market?' but 'is there a market in the gap?')

ACTION POINTS

- Set clear financial and service quality goals as medium and long term objectives.
- Calculate the break-even figure for your business.
- Calculate the Gross Profit Margin yielded by each type of service you offer for each target market segment in which you operate.
- Relate break-even to market trends and predictions. Make sure there are potentially enough customers to allow you to provide the service and make a profit. Calculate a range of prices, depending upon positioning in the market and the number of potential customers available within each target market segment.
- Decide the optimum positioning for each target market segment.

THE PLANNING GRID

The planning grid is a simple, yet powerful tool that enables easier strategic decision making, particularly when identifying directions for business development. The grid is similar to the one shown in Chapter 3 (Figure 3.2), which was used to illustrate segmentation and represented the example of Kate's printing business in the form of a matrix. An example is shown in Figure 4.1. Target market segments (customer types) are identified and listed along one side of a sheet of paper and types of service offered are listed along the adjacent side. For an existing business, the matrix is then formed showing which services are bought by which types of customer, but we now record the actual level of annual sales corresponding to each category, rather than just noting that sales exist. The final row and column are used to show the totals for each row or column, with the bottom right hand square showing the grand total representing all sales. For a new business start-up, the planning grid can be used to build up the picture of forecast sales expected in each category and to thus arrive at an overall sales turnover for, say, the first year.

Target customer	A	B	C	D	Total
Service					
1	£	£		£	£Y1
2	£		£		£Y2
3		£	£		£Y3
4	£		£		£Y4
5	£			£	£Y5
6			£		£Y6
					Grand Total
Total	£ X A	£ X B	£ X C	£ X D	£ X Y

Figure 4.1 *The planning grid*

The same planning grid can be used to record the results of market research, highlighting in particular the numbers of customers that make up the total possible market in every segment. Market share is the ratio of sales turnover achieved compared with the estimated total sales available in that segment.

Along with the sales figures recorded in each active segment, it should be possible to record the Gross Profit Margin achieved in each case. This analysis provides an extra dimension needed for strategic business planning, since some activities may yield high sales but low gross margin, and other parts of the business might yield lower sales but with each sale contributing a higher percentage gross margin.

Analysis of existing sales by breaking them out into relevant component segments in this way provides a pictorial representation of the business. This enables strategic direction decisions to be made more easily, although considerations of break-even figures needed and the actual capability of the organization must always be borne in mind.

DIRECTIONS FOR BUSINESS DEVELOPMENT

Market penetration

Expanding the level of sales of existing services to the existing types of customer who normally buy that service is known as market penetration and is probably the lowest risk strategy for growth. Although more staff and resources will be needed, no new skills need to be learned by the organization, other than those needed to cope with growth of the business. The GPM that can be expected will be known, as will figures such as profitability and ROCE, so risk can be assessed using knowledge already gained from providing the particular market segments with their particular services. The main area for concern will be maintenance and control of quality standards as the business grows.

The matrix formed in the planning grid by recording sales of existing services to existing types of customer also shows to which segments particular services are not being sold. Whilst the idea is not to try and fill every square in the grid, it is worth investigating which of the empty squares might hold further business development opportunities, and whether further types of customer, or service, might be successfully added to the grid.

There are only two ways of increasing turnover: find new customers (customers who are new to you and who may either be first-time users of a service, or ones whom you have attracted away from your competitors), or sell more to existing customers. And there are only two ways of selling more to existing customers: either sell them more whenever they buy, or get them to buy more often.

Market development

Expanding the provision of existing services into new market segments is known as market development. Expanding availability of the service to include customers in a larger geographic area is an example of market development. Some risk might be attached to this strategy since there is a temptation to assume that the new types of customer will be similar to existing types and that the same marketing message will be seen as being relevant. Thorough research, as already described, helps to minimize the risk of getting this part wrong. The marketing strategy is to promote the existing service in a way that is appealing to the new type of customer, although the service itself has not been changed. Financial expenditure will be needed to cover the cost of research and for implementation of the service to the new customers. A major consideration may be the employment of more staff and providing suitable training for them, as well as for head office staff dealing with an increased work load and different types of customer.

Service development

A generally accepted fact in business is that it can be at least five times easier and five times cheaper to sell to an existing customer than to find another new customer. Service development is the process whereby existing customers are sold new services (that is, services that are new to them from you). An example might be when an estate agent can provide facilities for obtaining a mortgage to customers buying a property through them, or a bank offers a range of insurance to its business account holders. Risks here may arise from too much diversification causing the organization to lose or dilute its strength in its core activity, drop its quality, or give cause to the customer to no longer value the service provider as a specialist in the original field of activity. Financial investment would be needed for new services to be properly tried, tested, and facilitated. Issues of staff training to provide the new services would need to be addressed. Both cash flow and overall profitability would therefore be reduced in the short to medium term.

Usually a service has to be continually modified, developed and up-dated in order to maintain its position within its existing market, as a process of on-going service development will be expected by ever more discerning customers. Care has to be taken not to try and expand through both market development and service development simultaneously, as this can weaken efforts within the core activity and cause management to 'take its eye off the ball' of the existing profitable operations.

Market research might identify opportunities for providing wholly new services to new customers. Entering such a market is basically a start-up situation and would thus carry the highest risk, since new skills and knowledge need to be acquired and the organization will be on a demanding new 'learning curve' to be able to quickly achieve the potential highlighted by the market research. In order to implement such a strategy, or indeed any type of expansion, a merger or acquisition might be considered. Some of the risks inherent in this approach were outlined in Chapter 3.

KEY POINTS

- The planning grid graphically represents the historical, or projected, sales matrix for a business.
- It can also be used to record market research results for each target market segment, and for noting the gross profit margin achieved from sales in each segment to identify the extra-profitable areas of business.
- Business development can be by way of market penetration (selling the same services to more of the same type of customer); market development (selling existing services to new types or location of customer); service development (selling new services to existing customers); or

start-up (selling new services to new customers). Each direction has to be considered on its merits, with an assessment of the inherent costs, risks and pitfalls.

● Developing in more than one direction at once can stretch an organization beyond the limits of its capability.

ACTION POINTS

● Construct a planning grid for your business.
● Record last year's sales relevant to each type of service purchased by each type of customer. (If your organization does not record sales information in this way, install a database system now to start doing it).
● Record market research results on the relevant parts of the grid.
● Record the gross profit margin you achieve from sales of each type of service in each target market segment.
● Consider possible profitable ways of developing your business through: market penetration, market development, service development, or new business start-up. Think 'outside the box'. Consider totally new (to you) services that you could provide to your existing customers, and consider totally new market segments that might be targeted with your existing services.
● Beware of overstretching your organization by trying to develop in more than one direction at a time.

VISION AND MISSION

Service businesses often find that they are asked to take on work that is outside of their main area of activity and may find it difficult to say no to such offers, on the basis that any work that provides turnover has to be accepted. However, over the longer term, businesses that have a clear idea of their purpose and goals are more likely to succeed and gain a good reputation for what they do best. A main cause of business failure for owners of business start-ups is not thinking through at the outset their personal and business objectives. A great deal of effort and thought often accompanies business development into new avenues, with little consideration given as to where that direction will ultimately lead the business, and what form an exit strategy should take for the individual owners.

It is 'vision' that motivates people and drives a business forward. Vision is about having challenging yet realistic and achievable ambition set within a defined time scale. It is a statement of the business's desired competitive position in, say, three, five or ten years' time, as far as can be guessed, as to what the future might hold. A vision statement states the aims of the business, which can be very helpful in guiding management and staff when they are faced with the need to make or interpret corporate policy decisions 'on the ground', as often happens within a service environment. An example of a published vision statement might be, 'XYZ aims to be the natural choice for ABC services throughout Europe.' The timescale set for such achievement might not be published, but would be known by staff throughout the organization.

Specific milestones need to be set so that the level of business success to date can be judged, and how far it has yet to go to reach the long term aims. These performance targets may be absolute, or relative to previous years, or relative to the position of competitors (which allows for unforeseen external factors), for example, 'We aim to increase our number of customers by 1,000 within 2 years.' 'We will increase our customer base by 25 per cent per annum over the next 12 months.' 'We will increase our market share by 2 per cent each year for the next 3 years.' Action plans can then be devised for each person within the organization to be able to work towards achieving each milestone. Achievement of milestones and, ultimately, of a vision statement, is great for morale within an organization and naturally leads on to the statement of further challenging vision positions.

It's not what you are that holds you back, it's what you think you are not!

A vision statement can be usefully accompanied by a statement of the organization's values and policies about the way it does things. It can be vital for a service business to ensure that all management and staff share common values. The fact that services are a 'people' business means that the corporate climate and culture should be conducive to satisfying and pleasing the customer. In a service business, it is often the originator's values and passion for the business that is a key ingredient for its success. When this pervades throughout the organization and is shared by every person in it, the customer can relate to the service provider on a personal and intrinsically more satisfying level.

A mission statement says what it is that the business does. It is a statement of purpose that guides the activities of the business. It also usually contains a definition of what market the business is in and a broad idea as to the type of customer the business aims to satisfy. An example of a mission statement might be: 'We provide prompt and efficient computer network solutions and installation services for small and medium sized business who value personal service at competitive prices.' Such a statement provides a coherent message about the nature of the business for employees, customers, suppliers, investors, etc. It also provides the necessary guidelines by which offers of work can be assessed to ensure that the business stays on a pre-determined course. It makes it easier to say 'no'! (If work has to be turned down, it is always useful to be able to divert that work to someone else within the firm's business network. It is often found that the network reciprocates the gesture at some later date.) If the nature and purpose of a business is not capable of being described in one sentence, it is probably because its mission has not been thought through, and this will make it very difficult to coherently market the service. In other words, if you cannot describe the nature and purpose of your business in one sentence, how do you expect others to understand what it does?

Directors or proprietors of many existing businesses may point out that they have never bothered about setting out vision, value or mission state-ments. Whilst this is true, they may still actually convey these concepts in other ways. And we will never hear from those businesses that failed for the want of clarity in their strategic direction decision-making!

KEY POINTS

- Businesses are more likely to be successful if they know where they are going.
- Businesses are more likely to be successful if directors, proprietors, managers and staff know where the business is going and are motivated by a common sense of purpose.

- A vision statement should set a challenging yet achievable long term aim.
- A vision statement provides a benchmark against which a firm can say 'no' to work that takes it away from its pre-determined route to success. It also prompts the subsequent question: What form should an exit strategy take?
- Milestones are short to medium term intermediate goals and targets to be achieved on the way to realization of the vision. Whereas a vision statement may be quite broad in character, targets along the way need to be specific and measurable. The team pulls together better when all members share common values. It is usually the originator of the business or its directors who determine the corporate culture – whether they mean to or not.
- A mission statement says what a business does. It is a statement of purpose that guides the activities of the organization and usually incorporates a definition of what market it is in and the type of customer it serves. It is another useful yardstick by which to say 'no' to the wrong type of work and allows management and staff to make and implement sensible policy decisions.

'Let's all pull in the same direction, at least!'

ACTION POINTS

- Write a vision statement for your business.
- Discuss it and share it with everyone in the organization.
- If you are the owner, consider where the business is taking you personally.
- Set milestones for the organization as a whole, and goals and targets for each individual within it.
- Decide what the corporate culture should be – and live it.
- Promote a commonality of values amongst everyone in the organization.
- Write a one-sentence mission statement.
- Discuss it and share it with everyone in the organization.

5

Pricing for profit

'The route to maximum profit is not through minimum cost.'

Pricing can be an emotive issue among service customers, yet it is vital that a business charges the right price to make a profit and ensure its continuing survival and capacity for growth and development. There is an old adage that says, 'Quality is remembered long after price is forgotten', and this can certainly be true for the service industry because of the transient nature of services. What remains in the customer's memory about a service should be the quality of it, perhaps the efficiency, promptness, or friendliness of the staff, etc. If the price is all that remains in the memory, then problems exist within the underlying design or delivery of the service.

Quality is intrinsically bound up with the concept of 'value for money'. From the customer's viewpoint, the price is part of their overall cost. The total cost reckoned by the customer can include their own estimations of the cost of their time and effort in availing themselves of the service, which they may well balance against the total cost to them of time, money and effort incurred by not availing of the service. 'Value for money' is a direct correlation between the benefits received and the cost incurred. The word 'price' does not enter into this definition of value for money. This is why the term 'perceived value for money' is sometimes used, since it acknowledges that the concept of value can only exist in the customer's perception. It acknowledges that the customer is buying the benefits of the goods and services that are being sold, not the goods or services themselves just for their own sake. A business might claim to offer a good price, but it is the customer who will decide the value.

Some of the issues surrounding pricing have already been raised in earlier chapters and pricing policy always remains a cornerstone of the marketing mix. However, it should not be allowed to be the dominant issue in a service context. Perhaps sales people need only two skills: to be able to sell, and to be able to come up with a good reason why they didn't! If a salesperson complains that a contract was lost to a competitor solely on price, perhaps it really means that the service was not being sold on its benefits to the customer, and that price was allowed to dominate an order-taking procedure, rather than a selling process. This may not be the sales-person's fault; marketing a service for profit cannot be achieved if the organization is actually buying customers, instead of selling the right services to the right customers at the right time and from the right location.

Where the price for a 'service' is not open to negotiation, as is the case for most facilities and utilities, the price charged is varied by the facility/utility provider according to the number of 'units of consumption' measured in quantity, time or distance. Because a service can be adapted to suit the requirements of the customer, it is more important for the service provider to think in terms of pricing structure, or pricing policy, rather than a simple fixed price. The price of a cup can be predetermined, but the price of serving tea in the cup depends upon when the tea is required, how quickly it is to be served, where it is to be served, the type of tea preferred, whether milk, sugar or lemon are wanted, whether it is to be served hot or as iced tea, where the water supply is, and whose facilities are to be used to make the tea! Consultants and other professionals generally do not have a fee, they have a way of calcu-lating their fee. The price for a service can be a matter for negotia-tion between the service provider and the customer, particularly as the customer is involved in the service process from the start and is often in direct communication with the service provider.

Whatever the circumstances, the price has to be seen as being fair to both parties, especially when repeat business is sought from the same customer or through word of mouth advertising. From the customer's viewpoint, fairness of price will depend upon the quality of the service – as perceived by the customer. From the business point of view, the right pricing structure for a service is that which best satisfies short, medium and long term objectives for the organization.

It is possible for a business supplying a lot of services in segments or locations that overlap to find that its pricing structure in one area is competing against its own offers in another area, cannibalizing some of its own efforts. Examples of this are sometimes noticeable in the passenger travel industry.

KEY POINTS

- Pricing can be an emotive issue, but businesses must price adequately to make a profit to ensure survival and development. The right price is that which best satisfies the business's short, medium, and long term objectives.
- The business may offer a good price for the level of service provided, but it is the customer who decides the value. If price is the customer's main memory, then the service was inadequate.
- If price is the dominant factor of the service offer, the other possible ingredients of the marketing mix have been neglected.
- Maximum profit from selling services can not be achieved by 'buying' customers through very low prices.
- Many service providers need a pricing structure, rather than a single 'fit-all' price.

ACTION POINTS

- Decide the short, medium and long term objectives for your business. These should be specific, measurable, achievable, realistic, and time-bound. (In other words, SMART).
- Ask some of your customers, or prospective customers, where they rank price in a list of six features about the type of service you offer. A typical list might include, say, location, your flexibility in service delivery, the fact that you offer a range of different service levels, speed/promptness of service, personal attention, as well as price.

- Remember that you are not your customer. Do not make any assumptions about what price your target customers are prepared to pay.
- Regularly follow up sales with 'open' questions to the customers, asking about their memory of the service.
- Identify the factors that will determine your pricing structure, for example, deadlines (theirs or yours), location, your objectives, your image, etc.

PRICING POINTS AND MANAGING CUSTOMER EXPECTATIONS

Pricing is only one element in the seven 'P's of the marketing mix and if attention has been paid to tailoring the remaining six factors in the mix, then probably what will matter to the customer about the price is how it relates to the expected 'pricing point'. The pricing point is basically the approximate maximum price that the customer expects to have to pay, and is usually related to a whole number figure such as, 'under £250'; or, 'less than £5'. The pricing point is never set in stone.

To a large extent establishing a pricing point is a matter of managing customer expectations. Customers of many different services, from washing machine repairs to packaged holidays, can often be heard to say, 'Of course it was more expensive than we had planned for, but we agreed [with the salesman] that it was well worth paying that little more for the extra warranty/comfort, etc!' Or perhaps, 'The estimate was £750, but the actual bill came to £728.'

Some customers do want to spend a lot of money on a service; either to ensure that they are getting the best, reducing/removing future risk, or perhaps to belong to an elite, to reassure investors or government inspectors, or for some other reason to be seen to be spending a lot of money. The apparent extra that is paid close to or over the pricing point is then the yardstick by which can be measured the extra quality, value or status received. The following notice to customers was seen printed on a piece of card pinned to the wall in the customer reception area of a busy repair business:

CAN IT BE GOOD, QUICK, AND CHEAP?

It may be quick and cheap – but it won't be good!

It may be good and cheap – but it won't be quick!

It may be good and quick – but it won't be cheap!

PRICING 'PACKAGES'

Where the sale is made up of component 'parts', such as providing a mixture of goods and services (for example, selling computers and installing them), or a number of service aspects are combined together (for example, mobile hairdressing), then the pricing can be structured in two ways. Firstly, an all-inclusive price that covers the whole 'package', or alternatively, pricing each 'component' separately.

The 'all-inclusive' price (which can be different for every customer) has the advantage of convenience for both the customer and the service provider, in that both parties know exactly what the outcome of the transaction is expected to be, in terms of benefits and the terms for payment. It also enables the service provider to choose whether to offer a nominal discount for any part of the 'package' not required by a particular customer. Such a discount will not necessarily reflect the price that would be charged for that aspect of the service if it were sold separately, but is sufficient for the customer to feel they have achieved a 'deal'. A 'packaged' price will probably make it more difficult for the customer to directly compare what is offered against the different 'packages' available from competitors.

From a practical point, the high ratio of fixed to variable costs that characterizes most services makes it difficult to correctly allocate costs between the various services provided and, as a business increases its range of services, job costing becomes increasingly arbitrary. In many cases there can also be a high level of interdependency between the various services provided. Both of these factors contribute towards price 'packaging', or 'bundling', which can particularly contribute to a firm's profit through economy of mutual administration systems for each component in the 'bundle'.

Sometimes the provision of a core service results in 'captive' customers for whom additional services can be obtained only from the original provider of the core service. This situation places the service provider in a strong position to charge high prices for the additional services. However, thought should be given here to the effects of such a strategy upon the image of the firm in the eyes of its customers, who may not have been aware of having become 'captive' at the time of their original purchase and may resent being 'held to ransom' without choice.

A 'package' strategy made up of non-negotiable separately priced components has been successfully used by the various mobile phone service providers in order to differentiate themselves in the marketplace. This has enabled them to lead their advertising with the lowest price/lowest risk aspect of their offer whilst preventing customers from comparing the relative merits and demerits of their prices on a like-for-like basis.

Just like buying a season ticket for rail travel, another example of an 'all-inclusive' price is when someone such as a counsellor, therapist, or beautician offers a programme or course of treatment over, say, three months. An 'all-inclusive' price can be quoted, which may allow some discount for advance booking since prepayment helps the business cash-flow. The usual way of pricing such services is to charge separately at each appointment, but by booking individual diary slots there is no guarantee (by either party) that a further booking is going to be made. The 'package' approach enables both parties to plan better and is more likely to build a stronger relationship. It also calls for commitment from both sides, and a good understanding by the service provider of what the customer really wants from the service.

An immediate disadvantage of the 'all-inclusive' method of pricing is that the price might appear off-putting as a headline figure, even though the benefits are stressed and it is emphasized that there are no 'hidden extras'. The customer may well expect some form of further service 'warranty' to allay their fear that they might not get everything that is promised in the 'package'. The concept of pricing-points and the ability to manage customer expectations are crucial here, as is the need to live up to those expectations.

The alternative, pricing each component separately, as with the daily train ticket or an hour's consultation as mentioned above, does not build planned repeat business into the transaction. It also implies that the business is more insecure and makes medium term forecasting for the business more difficult. Customers may only pay for what they feel they need, but pricing components separately can open the way for the customer to 'cherry pick' from the offer and will not necessarily allow the service provider to maximize profit unless the sale can be maximized. As mentioned in Chapter 1, insurance brokers selling individual insurance 'products' can only ever hope to earn the commissions on each individual product. And every aspect of a policy and every renewal of a policy requires a separate sales effort. Scrutiny of 'perceived value' is inevitably focused on the elements in the policy, rather than on the relationship between customer and broker.

Customers do not always realize the full benefit of a service until after they have experienced it. Allowing customers to cut short the intended level of involvement can make it impossible to ensure delivery of the full benefit required by the customer. This in turn can lead to damage to the service provider's reputation. For example, the computer seller might be wise to insist on seeing the equipment installed properly and thus avoid claims of malfunction or damage created by the buyer. Such claims would otherwise immediately rebound financially and, more importantly, cause loss of reputation as a supplier of good equipment and thus damage future business prospects. Likewise, the therapist's customer will never experience the real culminating benefit of the treatment if it is not delivered in a programmed way over a finite period of time.

KEY POINTS

- If the marketing mix has been correctly assembled, the target customer's limit on price will probably relate to a pre-conceived 'pricing-point', and this figure can be formulated by managing customer expectations. Customers do not expect to get something for nothing, but they do expect to get at least the level of service they pay for.

- Prices can be 'packaged' or 'modular'. That is, an 'all-inclusive' price can be charged, with discounts at less than cost perhaps being allowed for aspects that are not required, and 'unbolted', from the all-in price. Or a price can be calculated for each aspect of the service, so that prices for the various components are 'bolted on' to the core goods or service.
- Price 'packaging', or 'bundling', becomes more relevant as a profit generator as a business increases the range of services it offers. The high ratio of fixed to variable costs makes individual job costing difficult and the often interdependent nature of several services prevents separation and calculation of component costs.
- A 'packaged' price might at first glance appear expensive, but it enables the service provider to fully delight its customer through maximum involvement, building its medium/long term reputation.
- A 'packaged' price makes direct monetary comparison with competitors more difficult.
- Price 'packaging', or 'bundling', can make excellent financial sense where the ratio of fixed to variable costs is high and/or there is interdependency between services offered to the same target customer.
- 'Modular' pricing can offer a good 'lead-in' advertised price and enables customers to build up the service they perceive they want, but will only maximize profit if the service provider can sell them everything it wants to sell them.
- Allowing customers to buy the service 'short' may increase the risk of customer dissatisfaction and/or complaint and will almost certainly not allow the service provider the opportunity to fully delight them.

ACTION POINTS

- Make sure you are targeting the right type of customer.
- Make all aspects of the marketing mix attractive to that type of customer. The 'pricing-point' should become self-evident as a result of this process being based upon sound market and customer research.
- Consider what your customers actually want and then draw a flow-chart of the stages leading from your business to their objectives. Highlight any areas where you currently do not have control or the opportunity for involvement. Decide what you are going to do about these gaps in your ability to influence satisfaction for your customer.

- Explore the possibility of bundling components together to offer a 'package' of service to your customer. Apart from rationalizing the costing process, it might also allow you to improve the chances of customer delight, ask a higher overall price than if components were charged separately, or enable you to improve your income forecasting for the short/medium term.

THE 'GOING RATE' AND COMPETITORS' PRICING

The idea that everyone always pays the same amount for the same service can be an illusion. For example, holidaymakers staying at an hotel on the Mediterranean coast may have felt they had got a good deal from their travel agent, until they find out that nearly everyone else staying in the same hotel that week seems to have paid a lot less than they did! Of course, they may not be comparing like with like, but might still feel cheated by the travel agent or holiday company. Such customers have to be able to resolve their feelings in some way and this might be a task that the holiday company's representative in the area needs to deal with, if repeat custom is to be gained and the firm's reputation is to be maintained.

There may be a conventional wisdom that dictates that a 'going rate' is applicable. This is often true for the pricing of 'standard' services such as ordinary dry cleaning or the pricing structure for video rentals. In these cases, services may be price-sensitive, such that a small reduction in price might simply force competitors to lower their prices and no competitive advantage is gained. Likewise a small increase in price without any perceived increase in benefit to the customer will result in trade passing to competitors. Pricing for extra profit in these types of service, therefore, rests with adding value and pointing out to customers the benefits they gain from using the service instead of choosing the competitor's.

This also begs the question: who is the competitor? For example, an aromatherapist may be competing against, say, a beauty parlour or herbalist, as much as against other aromatherapists; video rental may be competing for customers' money that might otherwise be spent on going to the cinema, the theatre, or even a restaurant. The question really is: if my customers do not spend their money on buying my service, what else do they spend their money on?

A 'going-rate' is often used in arriving at a price for contract service work, in the case of most tradespeople, and in some types of technical or computer consultancy. The 'going rate' is generally applicable when a particular skill is sought by the customer, rather than a particular person or firm being asked to provide a service. To achieve extra profit when the 'going-rate' is based on an hourly rate or daily fee, the usual tactic applied by the service provider is simply to contract for extra time. What matters is the final charge, not the hourly or daily rate! When it is the particular individual or firm that is wanted, along with their skill, then the price charged can be higher. Sometimes the price commanded can be much greater and bears no resemblance to the normal price charged just for the skill, even allowing for excellence in quality.

An example of being able to command a much higher price is demonstrated by a famous violinist who had shot to fame after having produced a particularly brilliant recording of a piece of music. He exclaimed that after many years of performing, he was now being paid so much more money than before he had become famous, and yet he felt that neither he nor his skill had changed. He was delighted to be receiving so much money for doing what he loved doing (playing his violin) and he commented that he might be just as happy playing his violin in the street.

It is perhaps interesting to note, however, that if he were playing his violin in the street, people may stop to listen, and some might toss some coins into his violin case, but it would not have been a real concert. A real concert would be in the Royal Albert Hall, and cost £50 to be there! The irony is that the violinist could have been playing at his best in the street, and having an 'off' night at the Royal Albert Hall. This illustrates the fact that price is dependent upon the package, the augmented product, the total experience, and not just the skill involved. Many freelance service providers do the equivalent of 'playing their violin in the street' and do not necessarily consider the environment in which they could other-wise work, where they could do what they enjoy doing and be paid well for doing it.

The entertainment and music industries offer excellent examples of the application of the concepts of segmentation, targeting and positioning. In any service business, attention to these three stages will make all the difference to a company's profits. Price is dependent upon positioning and, to be successful, services offered by the service provider should appear to be the 'natural choice' for the target customer if there is a 'going rate' for that position in the market, in other words, the price is seen as fair.

When a potential customer seeks a service for the first time, price may be the only aspect they feel confident enough to ask about. Allowing the sales process to be dominated by this question devalues the service provider's position and in some respects takes the sales effort up a blind alley. What the customer will finally consider is not the price, it is the perceived value for money. This means that when other service providers normally offer the service at a particular price, or 'going rate', it is of course possible to gain a competitive edge in the market by undercutting them. However, this can backfire as potential customers may have concerns about the quality of the service they would receive. There is also the fact that customers who are buying on price alone have no other reason to remain loyal to any particular service provider. As soon as a different provider offers a lower price, those customers will take their custom to the new lower-priced service provider.

If instead, the emphasis is placed upon improving the number or value of the benefits the customer is to receive, then a competitive edge, or unique selling proposition, has been created. The customer perceives improved value for money without jeopardizing quality, a premium can be charged by the service provider, and the customer will acknowledge the need to pay more than their previously perceived 'going rate' for the basic service. Because price is not the dominant factor in the marketing mix and customers are buying for reasons other than price alone, customers have more reason to remain loyal to that particular service provider, as long as they continue to receive the quality that they appreciate.

Sealed-bid pricing

A sealed-bid tendering process is employed by many organizations seeking services to be supplied to them according to a predetermined specification. Service providers are aware that, particularly in the case of some national and local government contracts, the organization inviting the bids are often legally obliged to accept the lowest priced tender. Whether this is the case or not, bidders will be very conscious that pricing can be the deciding factor in gaining a contract, irrespective of any brand strength or loyalty they might have created for their services elsewhere in the market. The bidder has now to determine the minimum price for the contract, based upon its costs, and including a suitable charge to create their required profit margin and return on investment. The decision to bid higher than this figure will be largely based upon estimations of what competitors will bid.

The driving force behind sealed-bid tenders may be to drive down prices, but the desire by many service providers to gain contracts at almost any price can cause low quality services to be provided, resulting in loss of reputation or even financial failure, before the contract can be completed.

KEY POINTS

- Does a firm 'going-rate' really exist, or is it just a rough yardstick set by a real, or imagined, average service provider?
- Price is dependent upon positioning (just as positioning can be determined by price).
- A perceived 'going-rate' can only be applied according to the market segment and type of target customer involved, or when the service offer rests entirely upon the provision of a specific skill.
- A higher price can be commanded when the customer purposely requests your service, not just your skill.
- Pricing for extra profit usually means adding value to the offer.
- What matters to a business is the total price achieved rather than an hourly or daily rate, although it is often the hourly or daily rate that the customer thinks is of prime concern.
- When emphasis is placed upon adding value, then a competitive edge is established, which is more likely to keep customers loyal.
- Sealed-bid pricing has to be handled very carefully if maximum profit is to be obtained without jeopardizing reputation. It can tempt firms to quote a low price from which maximum profit is only achievable through subsequent non-delivery of promised quality.

- If entering into a sealed-bid proposal, it is wise to fully consider what the potential percentage return on investment will be, apart from just calculating the expected profit.

ACTION POINTS

- Decide your positioning in the market.
- Carry out sufficient market research to establish the parameters surrounding any apparent 'going-rate' in the market. Determine how these impinge upon your offer and what you are going to do about them.
- Add extra value to your offer, rather than being reliant upon selling only your skill.
- Calculate return on investment, as well as expected net profit, especially when undertaking sealed-bid pricing.

ALTERNATIVES TO COST-CUTTING

Cost-cutting by a service provider in order to increase profit usually becomes immediately evident to the customer since it invariably translates into a drop in quality of some sort. As a result, sales will decline as customers seek elsewhere to re-establish the quality to which they have become accustomed. An alternative strategy to increase profit can be implemented, however, by increasing prices and visibly improving service to justify the increase. This strategy will result in a fall in volume of sales, but the aim here is to chase profit, not volume. Because of the extra perceived benefits being provided, remaining customers have good reason to stay loyal to the service provider, as long as they continue to receive the improved service. Such customers may even act as unpaid ambassadors for the business if they feel that there has been a sufficiently significant improvement in quality of service. The real increase in profits, however, is from the cost savings brought about by the reduction in overheads that are now no longer needed to service the previously higher volume of customers.

By servicing fewer customers, the service provider now has more time in which to concentrate on delivering the service aspects of the business. Since time can always seem to be against the provision of good quality service, this point should not be overlooked. The risk inherent in adopting this type of strategy lies in the danger of 'placing all eggs in one basket', and over-reliance on a small number of large customers is best avoided. As a general rule, no more than 25 per cent of business should be with any one customer.

Purposely losing customers may seem like an act of folly, but it is worth doing the calculations to see what would happen to profits if prices were increased by, say, 10 per cent, and a resultant loss of volume is assumed at, say, 20 per cent, accompanied by a concomitant reduction in overheads. The calculations can be repeated for different 'what if' scenarios. Where goods are currently supplied to customers and the business appears to be dependent upon volume sales, it is worth the service provider considering whether to reposition at least part of the business towards specific target market segments that might already be amongst the customer base of the business, but that can be developed by adopting the above service-based strategy.

Research carried out by the service provider amongst its existing customers should indicate whether the proposed improvement in service, perhaps by more frequent deliveries for example, would be welcomed and whether the proposed increase in price would be accommodated. To remove associations with existing prices and methods of trading, a new 'package' of goods and services could be offered to existing and potential customers. This can be sufficiently differentiated from existing business by marketing the new 'package' under a special name, or by operating and marketing that part of the business under a different brand or trade name.

Trends within manufacturing have been towards 'just in time' deliveries of stocks. More frequent deliveries means a reduction in the customers' costs associated with stock-holding and both supplier and customer can gain from the new delivery arrangements. This strategy might be similarly applied to any business-to-business situation. Where perishable goods are involved, for example food products to retail outlets or restaurants, the benefit of more frequent deliveries to the retailer or restaurateur is fresher goods that might command a higher price to consumers, or that give the retailer or restaurateur an edge over the competition. In either case the retailer or restaurateur should be able to recover the increase in price paid to the supplier for the goods, either by charging their own customers a little extra or because their repeat business increases.

The 80/20 factor

This describes the fact that very often only about 20 per cent of a firm's profit comes from 80 per cent of its customers, whereas around 80 per cent of its profit originates from the remaining 20 per cent of its customers. These figures are not hard and fast, but do serve to indicate the need for the successful business to analyse not only what it is selling in financial terms, but to also analyse how its most profitable sales are being made and to whom. The idea is then to seek out more of the most profitable combination of customers and services. It is probably not possible to concentrate exclusively upon that group, since most firms need a flow of business 'traffic' for their bread and butter business and presence in the marketplace. Apart from which, many of the really profitable customers will originate in the '80 per cent' pool, buying the core goods or services before discovering the other 'packages' available.

KEY POINTS

- Customers will interpret evidence of cost-cutting as a diminution in the level of service the provider is willing to provide. The route to maximum profit is not through minimum cost.
- Extra profit can be achieved by re-positioning a service, adding value where the target customer appreciates it and is willing to pay more.
- This strategy may lose some of the customers for whom price remains the dominant factor, or who do not value the extra service to be provided. Being wary of not putting all eggs in too few baskets, the strategy is to increase profit, not turnover. Savings might then become available from reduction of overheads necessary to service fewer customers.
- Often there is disparity between volume of sales and percentage profit yield. The '80/20' factor operates in most businesses.

ACTION POINTS

- Consider your positioning in the market. Are you maximizing all the possible profit available from your resources? Can you re-brand or 'package' at least some of your services to appeal more directly to some of your chosen target customers?
- Analyse not only the financial information arising from your sales, but also the combination of type of customer and type of service that is yielding the greatest return on investment for you.

FACTORS THAT INFLUENCE PRICE

In some businesses, the profit is made when goods are bought and realized when they are sold. In other words, the emphasis is on buying or equipping at the lowest possible cost in order to make a profit and the required return on capital employed (for example, the over-expenditure on construction of the Channel Tunnel resulted in dire financial problems for its operators), as there is often a recognized resale price or rate of return that cannot be varied a great deal. Whilst this position may hold true for facility providers, generally service providers have to make their profit when they sell their services. As a principle cost of providing good quality services is often the payroll for employees, it can be self-defeating to try and pay low wages. Such a policy might be followed where the jobs are of low skill and out of direct contact with the customer, but few savings can be made on wages and training for staff and salaries for management of the calibre required for dealing with customers and delivering a quality service. It might, therefore, be assumed that there is little scope to make extra profit, since buying prices for consumables are probably much the same for all service providers and investment in overheads may be dictated by the needs of the customer.

To understand ways of pricing for profit, it is necessary to look at factors that go towards determining selling prices and ways in which the service provider might influence their selling prices. There are four basic factors that determine selling prices:

- the costs of producing and providing the service;
- any constraints on pricing that are imposed by government or other outside agencies;
- prices charged by competitors;
- what customers are prepared to pay.

The costs of producing and providing a service

As described above, unless a particular service provider has unique access to free or less-expensive resources, the costs of producing and providing a service will probably be much the same for all providers of comparable services. If the service provided is really just a facility provided to customers, then a temporary commercial advantage might be gained through using technology more efficiently than the competition. The ability to generate extra profit in this way is likely to be only temporary, until such time as competitors also use equal or better technology to make savings or force a price 'war'.

Alternatively, a service provider may rely on the use of older, established facilities that have already provided their initial return on capital employed. This minimum cost approach usually results in loss of turnover as customers move to use better facilities provided by competitors, or results in loss of potential profit caused by the inefficient facilities themselves, or because the less efficient facilities being offered cannot command a premium in the market.

Outside constraints placed on pricing

As described in Chapter 2, government may regulate monopolistic or near-monopoly service providers. It can perhaps also attempt to create a 'level playing field' by controlling prices, while making it easier for new players to enter a particular market sector, in order to encourage competition on the basis that lively competition will force down prices charged to the consumer.

Government can also lay down rules covering the representation of prices, particularly for services provided to consumers, in order to protect potential purchasers from misrepresentation or misleading sales techniques. Examples of such regulation can be found in the Consumer Protection Act and the Consumer Credit

Act, as well as in other Acts of Parliament designed to cover specific sectors where misrepresentation had been rife.

KEY POINTS

- For facilities, the opportunity for profit is generally created when the equipment or systems are installed and the return is realized as customers take up the service. With services, the opportunity to make profit is generally at the point of sale.
- The principal cost of providing a facility (equipment, systems, etc) is incurred at the outset, before revenue is earned.
- The principal cost of providing a service is often the on-going payroll for employees (or costs of contractors) but, since it is these people who are delivering the service, paying low rates can be self-defeating.
- Other ways can be found to increase profits, without jeopardizing quality of service.
- The factors that contribute towards determining the price are: the costs of producing and providing the service, any external constraints on pricing policy, competitors' prices, and what customers are prepared to pay.
- The costs of providing a service are probably similar for all providers of comparable services, although the use of technology may provide a (temporary) commercial advantage.
- Facilities require regular reappraisal and updating if a premium price in the market is to be maintained.
- External constraints (existing or likely) on pricing policy must be borne in mind.

ACTION POINTS

- Since services have a high ratio of fixed to variable costs, most expenditure, including wages, might be considered as investment in the business, with break-even, return on capital and 'payback' being calculated accordingly.
- Analyse each of the four factors outlined above, determining how extra profit can be made at the point of sale.
- Set a programme of regular facility appraisal to make sure you are safeguarding your position in the market.

The subject of prices charged by competitors and the 'going rate' have been dealt with earlier in this chapter. The fourth basic factor that can influence selling price is: what customers are prepared to pay. Some of the issues already raised inevitably impinge on this point and several reasons why customers might be prepared to pay more have already been described. However, what customers are prepared to pay can be extensively influenced by the service provider, particularly as the service provider can pre-decide the type of customer to be targeted. Within each target market segment there are four factors that will have a bearing on the best price achievable by the service provider:

● the demand for the service;
● the service provider's objectives, strategic choices and decisions;
● deadlines;
● location.

Demand for the service

The maximum price that can be obtained for a service is determined by what customers are prepared to pay for it. Different customers will have differing perceptions of value for money, depending on how the benefits of the service relate to their particular needs, so they will each put a different ceiling on what they are prepared to pay. Successful demand-based pricing is, therefore, based on effective segmentation of the available market by the service provider, to allow the maximum price for the service to be achieved from each segment. For many services, the identity of individual customers is known and the best possible price can be achieved through use of negotiating skills or 'tailoring' the service to exactly meet individual customer requirements.

Selling to organizations relies not on price but upon cost-effectiveness. Organizations buy for the benefit of eventually saving money, making money, or to transfer risk (recovering or saving possible future cost). The yardstick by which value is measured here is thus the comparison of price versus how much money the organization ultimately saves or makes by the deal. Since these figures will vary for every organization, the price charged may likewise vary. It is perhaps worth noting that, as a general rule of thumb, the larger the organization, the tighter is their margin of profit!

A pricing policy based upon demand can thus be implemented on the basis of differing demands arising from segmentation between different groups of customers, different times of use (deadlines), and different points of use (location). The transient (inseparable) and intangible nature of services mean that consumption of a service cannot be bought by a customer at a discounted price and sold on to a higher priced segment, as is possible in the purchase, storage and re-selling of goods. Tickets for an event might be sold on by intermediaries, but actual consumption of the event at the time it takes place cannot be stored and re-sold. This allows for price discrimination based on segmentation between different groups of customers. For example, public transport travel concessions allowed to senior citizens cannot be used by any other group of passengers and a club-class premium is charged by airlines for those customers wishing to fly in more comfort than offered by economy class.

The influence of demand can play a major role in determining what the customer might consider to be a fair, or necessary price. For example, a theatre or concert hall will vary its prices according to which play, act, ballet, musical, band, group, orchestra or soloist is performing. In most service sectors, a high or rising demand for a service will cause competitors to quickly enter the market. Many of these new service providers will simply undercut existing providers while there is the opportunity to do so and while the market is expanding. They ride the crest of demand and then disappear, or their facilities are perhaps bought by larger players in the market. Examples of such tactics were evident during the booms in home video rental services and mobile phone retailing.

When the competition appears to be there to stay, new ways of receiving payment for services might be contemplated. Finding new ways of receiving payment enables the service provider to break away from conventional charging policies that are causing prices to be forced down just to enable the provider to remain competitive. An example of this is the way that charges for Internet access have moved away from individual billing and towards sharing of profit generated by the provider of the line. The pricing and marketing implication is that the service can be described by the provider as being 'free'.

In similar examples, some service providers, particularly if they are conveyors of information, have expensive call rate telephone numbers as a way of gaining payment from enquirers. Likewise, hotels and similar establishments have for many years added their own margin on to the cost of using telephones provided in guests' rooms. As technology develops, more and more opportunities will arise for innovative payment schemes to be brought into use.

The earlier story about the violinist was an example of price being influenced by demand. However, the ability to charge a higher price does not rest solely with becoming famous or being brilliant. Being in demand may arise through astute public relations, advertising and promotional activity and this facet will be discussed later (See Chapter 6: Targeted promotional strategies). Demand for a firm's services should also arise as a consequence of correct positioning, by being the 'natural choice' for target customers. An interesting example of this was illustrated by the newly qualified architect who decided that he would start his own practice, specializing in designing and building hotels for clients. His father had been a builder who had developed a reputation for hotel renovation, conversion and construction, so the son felt comfortable within that market.

The first thing that he did after setting up his studio was to buy a red Ferrari (on hire purchase). Of course, his colleagues and friends jibed that he would be either viewed as a playboy rather than as a professional architect, or that prospective customers would assume that his fees were excessive. In the UK they would probably have been proven right. However, he was proven to have done the right thing when enquiries for his services came in from Bahrain, Kuwait, the United Arab Emirates, etc. The Arab investors in hotel properties respected the qualifications of any British architect, but they also concluded that their multi-million dollar hotels, with marble fountains and gold bathroom fittings, would be best served by this British architect who drove a red Ferrari. He matched their sense of style – he was the natural choice! And his architect's fee for one such hotel alone was probably enough to buy several Ferraris.

Pricing can be used to regulate demand downwards, as well upwards. Excess demand can be trimmed by increasing the price, although for some sought-after service providers (for example, those selling a high status service), a rise in price may actually encourage custom.

The service provider's objectives

Unfortunately for most businesses owners, buying a Ferrari is probably not the solution to marketing their services for profit! The concept of positioning is however, and this theme will run through successive chapters of this book. What is also relevant to pricing policy are the objectives of the service organization and its owner(s). For the freelance service provider, perhaps the objective is to earn enough to replace the annual salary previously earned from an employer. If we take an example of someone setting out to replace a salary of, say, £30,000, then first we must take into consideration the fact that the salary also included holiday pay, sick pay, and probably contributions towards an occupational pension scheme. This means that the figure of £30,000 must be uplifted by some factor that takes into account these items, since they will each now need to be covered out of the freelance earnings. This factor might be, say, a third or a half more, so the freelance earnings might have to be one and one-third to one and a half times £30,000, which brings the total, before tax, to around £40,000 to £45,000 per annum.

For someone who has been on a salary of £30,000, it may be difficult for them to convince themselves that they might now be worth around £45,000 per annum, but for an employer, even as an annual total, this figure may be less than the real cost of employment after sick pay, holiday pay, Employer's National Insurance contributions, training, staff development and other overheads are also taken into account. The advantage of using a freelancer is of course that the 'employer' can tailor costs directly in line with their need for the service.

Next to be considered is the time frame in which the money can be earned. Deducting the days in the year when one perhaps cannot earn, such as Bank Holidays and weekends, and allowing some time for holidays, business administration, continuous professional development, domestic cares and crises, sickness, etc, probably leaves the average freelancer just over 225 days in which to earn their money. It is highly unusual for a freelancer to have every available day booked by fee-paying clients; 'when you are earning you are not selling, and when you are selling you are probably not earning'. Assuming that the freelancer obtains fee-paying work for 150 days (an optimistic two-thirds of the available days), the average daily fee rate that has to be charged is easily calculated from £40,000 to £45,000 divided by 150 days, which equates to £267 to £300 per day. Earning fees for only half of the available days means that the daily fee rate must be in the region of £355 to £400.

Redundancy and the trend towards 'retirement' from employment at age 50 has created an ever-growing group of freelance professionals wishing to remain commercially active. If they are themselves financially secure, there can be the temptation to grossly under-price themselves because, 1) they 'do not need the money; 2) because they lack the confidence that comes with experience of negotiation; 3) they have not carried out proper research into what could be available. The result is that the benefit of the individual's lump sum and/or pension is being passed straight to the 'employer' of their services, whilst the individual (initially at least) feels 'grateful' for the work!

Strategic choices and decisions

From the viewpoint of an organization's objectives, pricing may be determined by different stages in a marketing plan as a new service is rolled out, or as customers are attracted away from competitors. Irrespective of other segmentations within a market, the development of sales passes through five types of customer. The first to take up a brand new service are termed 'innovators' and comprise people and organizations who like to be at the forefront of new developments, either to be seen as trendsetters, or in an attempt to gain competitive advantage for their own business. The second group to take up a new service is comprised of 'early adopters' and these are followed by many others as the 'early majority'. The 'late majority' follow when the service is fully established and proven. Finally the 'laggards' will take up a service only when it has become fully integrated into the market, its price has dropped and it has become a normally accepted part of social or business life. Pricing will play an essential part in the positioning of the service in the market if the optimum number of customers is to be attracted during each of these predictable phases of sales development.

Price skimming is the term applied when a relatively high price is charged to quickly recover set-up costs. The customers targeted will be the 'innovators', those who like to be amongst the first to try a new service. Price skimming can also arise where the service provider holds a monopoly or near-monopoly of supply and customers have little choice of service provider. A policy of price skimming when a brand new service is brought to the market will encourage competitors to start up also, attracted by the opportunity.

As competitors enter the market, prices are reduced. This can cause problems with customers who have paid the higher price and does not help that company's attempts to be seen as always having its customers' best interests at heart. By allowing the opportunity for competitors to enter the market, the original firm may then always have to compete harder and thus the short-term price skimming gain may be countered by loss of longer term volume and profit. Pricing strategy has to be considered carefully if the objective of the service business is to gain maximum market share, in order to achieve economies of scale and a competitive advantage from which maximum profit might then be obtained.

Customers are not naïve, in that they know that commercial services must make profits. While genuine improvements in customer facilities or services are seen to be taking place, little attention seems to be paid to the service provider's margins. But once an organization provides a reason to be mistrusted, or customers feel that they have been taken for granted, customer loyalty cannot be assumed by the organization. Indeed, many customers will actively seek an alternative service provider or simply stop using the service.

Getting customers to try a service for themselves is the most vital part of the whole business process. Once an initial trial has been made, the service provider can seek to develop loyalty from the customer, building repeat business and word of mouth advertising. As a result of increased loyalty, existing customers may be prepared to pay progressively increasing prices for the service. This becomes especially evident when a new service relies for its success upon a large initial uptake in order to make the service even more attractive to its users. For example, the larger the audience, the more satellite television broadcasting can expand to offer a wider range of programmes and justify progressively increasing prices.

Tactical pricing can be used to create short-term competitive advantage. Whether the service is new or established, periodic price reductions can be offered to induce potential customers to try the service for their first time, or encourage lapsed users to return. Likewise, a price reduction can be used to remove unplanned or 'off-peak' excess supply occurring either within the firm, or the market in which it operates. Price reductions for a limited period can be applied across-the-board, or targeted, perhaps through the use of vouchers. In either case, it is a good idea if a specific reason for being able to make the reduction can be publicly linked to the offer. Without a rationale and thought-through advertising, customers could be left wondering if the service is normally over-priced or that quality has been sacrificed.

Tactical price reductions are sometimes used by larger service providers to protect markets against new entrants. Where a new entrant threatens to take customers from an established provider operating in a price-sensitive market, the latter may react with a short term price reduction to put pressure on the new entrant to withdraw. When faced with threats to 'their' market following the deregulation of bus services in the UK, some established bus companies ran 'free' buses ahead of their new rivals.

If a service provider has no unique selling proposition and is seeking to enter a market as a copy of an existing successful player in that market, then the strategy known now as 'saturation pricing' is often used. The newcomer starts by offering a low price to switch customers from the original service provider, and will particularly attract customers who have no brand loyalty to that firm. Undercutting is sometimes used as a means of getting on to a commercial buyer's list. Once customers have been gained, their loyalty may be developed and prices slowly increased. The process of gradually increasing prices may succeed in particular when the customer is not sure how the charges are constructed, or is unsure as to whether there is a 'going rate' and, if so, which 'going rate' applies to them. The process also relies to an extent upon the lethargy of the customer, an unwillingness or reluctance to keep changing service providers, or their perceived inability to do so.

The risk to the service provider of adopting a saturation pricing policy is that customers may indeed show no brand loyalty at all and be just as ready to switch to the next competitor who offers lower prices. There is thus no opportunity to recover extra profit from the exercise. Further, service quality will presumably be hard to implement or sustain at reduced prices and customers may quickly become dissatisfied and move on, leaving the service provider with a reputation for poor quality and the inability to retain its customers.

Where a service provider's objective is to offer a range of services, there is usually a core service and the others are 'optional extras' for the customer. The extra services not only enable the customer to tailor the overall service to suit their needs, but also provide useful sources of extra profit for the service provider. The price of the core service may be the only price that is taken into account by customers, or is perhaps the benchmark price reported by the media in 'league tables' of prices gathered to try and compare value offered by each of the main players in the market. The lead-in price for the core service is not a loss-leader, yet it is low enough to make the service provider appear keenly competitive. Examples of this strategy can be found throughout the financial services industry, the travel industry and car servicing market. (See also 'Pricing packages' described earlier in this chapter).

To achieve a foothold in a particular target market, or perhaps with one potentially large customer, it is tempting for the service provider to contemplate employing a 'loss-leader' tactic. This is particularly prevalent amongst first-time freelance service providers who are not sure of themselves, or who feel they are on a learning curve and cannot justify a higher charge. Sometimes a firm simply needs the cash flow to survive and may resort to 'buying customers' just so that it can hold together its team of people until times improve, or until perhaps the next large contract can be negotiated.

Some customers or clients may be on the lookout for each of the above situations and may hold out a promise of future opportunities and contacts to follow if the first service project is provided at a low price. This can particularly arise when the prospective customer knows that it is influential or prestigious. It is necessary for the service provider to make a pragmatic decision at this point as to whether a trade-off is likely to occur and whether to succumb to the pressure to reduce its normal price.

Where a service is priced according to time taken, that time can never be replaced and lost profit cannot be recovered from that customer or client unless another, more expensive, service is provided as well. The problem with reducing the price for a service is that it is hard to restore it to the correct level next time. This can also affect negotiations with prospective clients/customers if most of the service providers' work arises from referrals, or word of mouth. The reduced price may be communicated by the past client/customer on to the prospective one, who will not expect the price to be higher for them. We have also seen how price is interwoven with the customer's perception of quality, so it is hard to maintain a quality image if the price can be readily reduced. An over-readiness to 'horse-trade' can appear to also conflict with a professional's integrity. There are possible solutions to these sorts of pricing problems and they will be covered later in this book.

Once a relatively new service provider starts to become a little more established in a market, the new customers will comprise the 'early adopters' as mentioned earlier. This group is likely to have been influenced in its decision to try the service by the 'innovators' and by further promotional activity. Pricing strategy forms a coherent part of the marketing mix throughout the sales development process and is a key indicator for the positioning of the service in the market. The early adopters may be prepared to pay as much as the innovators, but will often know from having experienced the introduction of other new services that the price may come down as a new service gains ground. They may thus prefer further inducement to encourage them to try the service at an early stage.

The 'early majority' of customers start to buy as the price drops and the service has been sufficiently proven to enable them to assess any risk. It is often at this point that competitors crowd into a market, hoping to capitalize on the groundwork that has been established, and usually offering reduced prices in order to gain market share. The 'late majority' of customers will wait until the price has fallen sufficiently, the service has proven itself thoroughly, and the market has reached maturity. A number of less-successful competitors will have disappeared by this time and the market will appear quite stable. It is only after a service has become a social or business norm that the laggards will buy the service. This group of customers may well be prepared to pay the same price for the service as the late majority if it feels that the price has reached its lowest 'going rate', although further inducement to first try the service may be needed.

Deadlines

As indicated earlier, prices for services can be raised or lowered on the basis of segmentation by time of consumption, and the time when a service is required is a dimension in which the overall demand exists. Services often face peaks and troughs of activity, caused by fluctuating demand over time. Levels of business may, or may not, follow predictable patterns that may, or may not, be within the control of the service provider. The pricing of services to achieve optimum profit depends to a very great extent upon anticipating and satisfying deadlines.

At the height of a peak in demand, higher prices can usually be justified as customers are willing to pay more, and higher costs may arise for the service provider in catering for the temporary increase in demand. During periods of low demand, prices may be relaxed, especially if the service provider's overheads have been already covered and only a marginal cost is incurred to provide the service to a small number of customers. Also, discounted pricing in this context can be used in an attempt to even out consumption of the service, although it is only relevant to that segment of customers for whom time is not the main consideration.

Deadlines affect pricing decisions for both goods and services. For example, certain consumer goods will be highly priced before Christmas and then perhaps dramatically reduced immediately afterwards. Services are often likewise in demand because of a deadline that exists for both the customer and the service provider. The year 2000 computer 'bug' proved a dramatic influence on both demand for specific computer services and the prices that could be commanded by those service providers who had the necessary skills to help resolve the problems. Similarly, prices for services required during the evening of the millennium celebrations could be 'skimmed' by almost every type of service provider involved, fuelled by 'wage price' skimming by employees of service providers!

When a commonly acknowledged deadline does not exist, then

either the customer's deadline or the service provider's deadline may exert a strong influence on price. How a service provider prices according to a customer's deadline is decided by the nature of the service provider's mission and strategic approach to the market. For example, a courier operation that targets customers needing urgent parcel and document deliveries will have already built into its pricing the urgent nature of the work it receives and customers will be aware of this before contacting it.

A further surcharge for speed of service would not be expected unless, perhaps, the delivery was of an especially vital and extremely urgent nature. To accommodate such cases, the service provider will have chosen whether an extra charge is to be applied or whether the delivery is considered to be an example of how that business can be of assistance to its customers. To prevent abuse of the service, the decision not to charge a premium may only apply to regular customers who do not normally ask for such a service. The decision not to charge extra might thus be used to build the relationship with the customer to try and ensure continuing and future custom, and to prevent the customer from sampling a competitor's service.

In many towns, the corner shop has been replaced by the convenience store. Certainly such shops are convenient for a great many regular customers, some of whom perhaps are not able to travel elsewhere. But they also attract custom from people who use them only when they have a deadline, perhaps when they have run out of some essential item in the evening for example. In either case, prices charged for goods in convenience stores generally reflect the fact that, for many people, time has a price.

A car driver needing some engine oil late at night found the price of oil to be much higher at the local all-night garage. When the customer commented that the oil was priced significantly higher than at the local auto-discount store, the garage assistant suggested that the driver should buy the oil from the auto-discount store. The customer pointed out that it was closed, to which the reply came: 'Well, our oil is much cheaper when we're closed!'

Customers' deadlines may be the underlying reason for peaks in demand for certain services, such as rail travel. For commuters, the need to arrive at work by a certain time each morning creates the rush hour and the price of their rail journey is increased accordingly. Outside of the rush hour and at weekends, the rail service provider has to reduce dramatically fares to induce passengers to use the service. Other examples of pricing according to customers' deadlines might be seen in banking services, where a premium is charged for the express clearance of a cheque, and in emergency repairs requiring call-out of a tradesperson such as a plumber or electrician. Meeting a customer's deadline is usually expected as part of the quality of a service; exceeding a customer's deadline can make a big difference in the relationship and help to secure repeat business.

Of course, when it is the service provider who has the deadline then the prices charged may be much lower. As described earlier in this chapter, a firm in need of cash flow may not be able to afford the luxury of a varied pricing policy and may offer markedly low prices just to get cash in so that it can survive a little longer.

Location

Service organizations can often charge premium prices by virtue of the location or point of consumption of the service. The point of consumption at which a service is used is a further dimension in which overall demand exists, and represents a further means of demand/price segmentation. For example, the convenience store and the garage forecourt retail shop can often charge higher prices than a supermarket because of the convenience of their location as well as the convenience of their opening times. A location that is convenient for the customer can often command significantly higher prices for services than one that is less convenient. Remembering that the customer's perception of value for money is arrived at by comparing benefits against total cost, a convenient location may significantly lower the cost of travel and/or time that the customer might otherwise incur in order to have the benefit of the service.

The basis for the prices charged by an hotel is largely influenced by the benefit of the location that it offers. The price of a return flight to Dublin from Birmingham can be very different from that charged for essentially the same return journey, yet flying from Dublin to Birmingham. Likewise the cost of similar journeys to and from Manchester will be different again, even if the same aircraft is used and the distance might be comparable. The cost of flights to and from London will be structured according to the higher demand to and from that location, tempered only perhaps by the possible presence of more competitors.

Location may also play a large part in the concept of perceived value for money. If a customer is seeking 'the best', one only has to consider the Swiss clinic, the Harley Street doctor, or solicitors in prestigious city centre offices, to also realize that the location of a service can contribute to an image that commands a high price. Again, we might consider the violinist mentioned earlier. The dominant reason for customers being prepared to pay a higher price was simply the Royal Albert Hall location in which the service was to be provided, i.e. the quality and perception of value for money (benefits) may be vested as much in the location and sense of occasion as in the performance itself.

A well presented Web site can put even the smallest service provider working from home on an apparent even footing with the largest player in the market when potential customers are scanning the Net. Prices need not be published, since the main job of the Web site is to get the prospective customer to contact the business and price may be a function of location where the service is to be delivered or otherwise provided. Once the dialogue is underway, a right time to discuss price becomes apparent.

KEY POINTS

- The maximum price that can be obtained for a service is determined by what customers are prepared to pay for it. This can be extensively influenced by the service provider who chooses the target customers.
- The four factors having a bearing on what the customer will pay are: demand, the service provider's own objectives, deadlines, and location.
- For many services (rather than facilities), the identity of the customer is known, so there is the opportunity to negotiate the most profitable outcome.
- A high demand can command a higher price, although it will also encourage new entrants into the market.
- New ways of receiving payment may enable the service provider to break away from conventional charging policies and remain profitable whilst still offering a financial-based advantage to its customers. More innovation in this aspect of pricing can be expected as technology advances.

- Astute public relations, advertising and promotional activity can dramatically increase demand.
- The service provider's objectives are a good starting point when considering what price ought to be charged.
- New services coming on to the market pass through five stages of the market's 'life cycle' and each stage is characterized by a different purchasing psychology on the part of customers who are represented as: the innovators, the 'early adopters', the 'early majority', the 'late majority' and the 'laggards'.
- Different pricing tactics to maximize profit can be applied at each stage of the market 'life cycle'. Care must be taken to ensure that pricing forms part of a coherent marketing mix and that a pricing strategy for short term profit does not damage longer term prospects (assuming an objective is to remain in the market over the longer term).
- There should be a good (public) reason for any price reduction offered.
- It is sometimes possible for short term price reductions to be used to 'see-off' new entrants who are challenging for market share.
- New entrants may themselves adopt an initial strategy of very low prices in order to get a foothold into the market. Their prices must inevitably rise, albeit stealthily.
- A 'loss-leader' tactic needs to be thoroughly thought through, since it is hard to increase prices once they are established and some buyers will be on the lookout to take advantage of the novice's willingness to under-price their first job.
- Price and perception of quality are inextricably linked.
- Time is an integral part of a service offer. The pricing of services to achieve optimum profit depends to a great extent upon identifying or anticipating and satisfying customers' deadlines or need for immediate attention. Being reliable and exceeding a customer's deadline can make a big difference in the relationship, delight the customer, and help secure repeat business.
- Location or point of consumption of the service can influence the price the customer is willing to pay and can be used as a basis for tactical price setting to optimize profits. It is a contributing factor towards the public image of the business and thus influences a customer's expectation about likely price.

ACTION POINTS

- Understanding your customers includes understanding their views about pricing and from whom they may have bought similar services in the past.
- If you have doubts about your negotiating or selling skills, sign up for a training course or delegate these responsibilities to trained professionals.
- Blend your price into your offer as part of a coherent marketing mix aimed at the right target customer. Identify the parameters that you will use to control your pricing structure and what stage in its 'life cycle' your market has reached.
- Undertake any price reduction tactics with a great deal of care and forethought, keeping an eye on competitors to try and anticipate movements in the market. Always state a good reason for why your price has been reduced.
- Be aware of how time, timeliness and speed of service can influence your reputation, and therefore, your price.
- Consider the relative merits and drawbacks of changing the location from which you operate.
- Ask customers for their opinion of your Web site.

6

Targeted promotional strategies

'It's easier to sell happiness than to buy it!'

Commercial advertising and promotional activities are the communication tools by which companies capture the interest of potential customers, and then keep their interest alive. For service companies, these activities do not in themselves sell anything. They inform, describe, question, reassure, allay fears, advise, and to some extent persuade customers to make contact with the service provider. It is this contact that allows the buying stage of the transaction to take place.

CUSTOMER EXPECTATIONS

Advertising and promotional activities stimulate the customer's expectation. Advertising is a form of promise and as such the consequences are worse if that promise is broken than if it had never been made. That is, if the customer's experience fails to live up to their reasonable expectations, feelings of disappointment, frustration, even anger, will result. The previous chapter introduced the concept of quality being remembered long after price has been forgotten and people's memories are made up of stored emotions. Services are intangible and transient; unlike goods

Target your customer

which can continue to exist into the present, all that remains of a service is a memory of it and whether it lived up to expectation.

Businesses generally get the customers they deserve.

TRIGGERS

Chapter 3 described how people buy goods and services as a way of solving problems they have, to satisfy emotional and/or physical needs. An implication of this is that customers will not contact a service provider until they recognize that they have a need, or they anticipate that they will have a need. That is, there must be some sort of 'trigger' that makes the customer actually initiate the possibility of a sale. The trick is to identify the triggers that can set the selling process in motion. As described in Chapter 3

(Problems? What problems?), triggers are often obvious, yet sometimes quite subtle.

As an example of linking to an obvious trigger, builders can look through the local applications for planning permission to identify who might need their services. Likewise, function caterers can scan the engagement notices published in the local press to identify possible future wedding receptions required. Accountants seeking prospective clients can identify new business start-ups in the area through networking, or just by looking out for their advertising in shop windows or the local newspaper. Painters and decorators, shop or office fitters, telecommunications or computer installers, and a whole raft of other service providers can respond to 'Sale Agreed', 'Sold', or 'Let' signs appearing outside commercial premises. Milk deliverers and other tradespeople can do likewise when they see these signs appearing outside properties in their sales territory. Ceramic tilers, plumbers and electricians can develop their contacts with suppliers and fitters of new kitchens or bathrooms. Travel companies can anticipate customers' needs to travel to a forthcoming special event.

THE MARKETING PROCESS

Anticipating the trigger that can lead to a sale is at the heart of targeted marketing. Remembering that the marketing process relies upon first segmenting the market enables the service provider to identify the type of customer sought, and the reasons why those potential customers might need the service on offer. Targeting the prospective customer identifies when specifically the service might be needed. The third stage of the marketing process is positioning the service offer to be attractive to the prospective customer, being 'the natural choice' (see Chapter 3). Positioning is the 'why will they buy from me?', as well as the 'what?' and 'how?' of the process.

Chapter 3 compared finding good customers to the process of going fishing: first decide the type of fish you want to catch (and whether it is plentiful and why you think it is possible to be caught), then identify the best place to catch it and when the best time is to catch it (in this case it is probably when the fish is hungry or curious!), finally you attract it using the right line bait and hook (and/or groundbait to get it interested). The aim is to catch one fish at a time. You are not trying to catch all types of fish all at once.

The Planning Grid described in Chapter 4 (Figure.4.1) identifies the types of customer you are aiming for, together with what it is that you are intending to sell to each type. This information is essential if you are to establish the best ways of attracting, catching and keeping customers. Varying the marketing mix to match the customer's needs enables any service provider to position themselves to be attractive to the type of customers that they want. Just advertising blindly may result in volume, but will most likely not achieve the customers you want; indeed, you may also end up with the 'customer from hell'! Advertising indiscriminately, through the wrong media, with wrongly worded content, or at the wrong time, can not only waste a tremendous amount of money, but can result in catching less profitable customers.

The customer from hell

COMMON SERVICE MARKETING FAILINGS

As previously mentioned in Chapter 2, the actual quality of a service becomes directly relevant only after a customer has committed to pay for it, so before that time it is purely the quality of the marketing that determines success. Many service companies are very competent at what they do, yet they have only the promise of their skills or services to sell. The most common failing within service based businesses is poor marketing. Below is a list of some of the common causes of poor performance, and perhaps inevitable failure, for many service based businesses:

- Not being identified by the customer as providing a possible solution to their problem at the time that they need it.
- Not offering a 'unique selling proposition' (USP) that differentiates your offer from your competitors. (USP might also stand for Unambiguous/Unfailing/Universal/Unilateral Service Promise).
- The inability or unwillingness to communicate in terms relevant to the customer, for example, the computer consultant intricately describes in computer jargon the mechanics of some new computing wizardry, rather than saying, 'This system will save you a great deal of the time and money you currently spend on your admin work and filing, and is flexible enough to meet your needs for the future.' (See Chapter 3: Features, advantages and benefits – and the ultimate benefit').
- Not defining the types of customer (market segments) to be targeted, and not targeting them, that is, believing that all that has to be done is to set out a stall somewhere and customers will appear.
- Not focusing on one type of target customer at a time, that is, trying to be all things to all people all at once.
- Not positioning the service offered in a way that is most attractive to that customer, and at a price that is not cheap.
- Trying to maintain a catch-all position even when talking to each individual potential customer.
- Not promoting themselves with consistency and regularity, for example, returning to pitch for customers only when the business is desperately needed, and by then even their original network of contacts have forgotten them, or moved on.

- Not being honest and direct with customers.
- Not listening to existing customers, or not heeding what they are trying to tell you. Not 'looking after them'.
- Relying on only one major customer or contract and not keenly cultivating the next generation of customers.

KEY POINTS

- Commercial advertising and promotional activities are the communication tools by which companies capture the interest of potential customers, and then keep their interest alive.
- For service companies, they inform, describe, question, reassure, allay fears, advise, and to some extent persuade customers to make contact with the service provider.
- It is this contact that allows the buying stage of the transaction to take place.
- Advertising and promotional activities stimulate the customer's expectation.
- Advertising is a form of promise.
- The consequences are worse if that promise is broken than if it had never been made.
- Quality is remembered long after price has been forgotten.
- All that remains of a service is a memory of it and whether it lived up to expectation.
- Businesses generally get the customers they deserve.
- A trigger initiates a customer's need to buy; the trick is to identify the triggers.
- Anticipating the trigger that can lead to a sale is at the heart of targeted marketing.
- The three stages of service marketing are: segmentation, targeting and positioning.
- The Planning Grid identifies the types of customer to be aimed for, together with what it is that each is forecast to buy.
- Varying the marketing mix to match the customer's needs enables any service provider to position themselves to be attractive to the type of customers that they want.
- Just advertising blindly may result in volume, but will most likely not achieve the type of customers wanted.
- Many service companies are very competent at what they do, yet they have only the promise of their skills or services to sell.

- The most common failing within service based businesses is poor marketing.

ACTION POINTS

- Check your advertising or promotional message. Is it still relevant?
- Does your company always keep its advertising promises? What is the memory left with your customers? Contact them and find out.
- Identify the obvious triggers that initiate the customer's purchase.
- Explore the less obvious triggers that might be operating.
- Construct a Planning Grid and use it.
- Consider what might happen if the marketing mix is varied.

REACHING NEW CUSTOMERS

Some ideas have been provided as to the triggers that might initiate a prospective sales call, and each service provider will need to identify for themselves the triggers that might result in sales enquiries to them from the types of customer that they want. Prospective target customers can be reached directly or indirectly. Indirect tactics may take longer to gain the response you require, but can be extremely effective in the long run. Direct targeting means conveying your message directly to your target customer, either by 'cold calling' or through the use of an advertising medium. Perhaps the first aspect to consider is how to convey the message successfully.

CONVEYING YOUR MESSAGE

This section looks at how you might best communicate your details to your chosen prospective customers, so that they convey the right message, the right image, and customers have them to hand when they need them.

Advertising and promotion

Often the immediate thought is of media advertising, printed business cards, leaflets, brochures, timetables, etc. Firms providing repairs to equipment often leave labels stuck on to the equipment to provide the customer with immediate access to their call-out number. Business cards can be laminated to keep their appearance sharp and clean, as well as making them distinctive. Leaflets and brochures can be designed for easy recognition and of a size that makes them easy for the recipient to store for later reference. Regular trade press advertising, being listed in directories and having a Web site also make contact details easily obtainable. Likewise free gifts, such as key fobs, pens, coffee cup coasters, bookmarks, etc can keep your contact details in front of the customer as long as they use the item. Free gifts might also be in the form of information products that carry other useful information as well as your details, and so are likely to be kept for the information they convey. Examples of information products are diaries, tax tables and figures, metric conversion charts, useful telephone numbers or Web site addresses, timetables, tidetables, maps or guides, etc.

Any approach to a prospective customer will convey an image of your business. You have an image; it is a matter of how you control it. In each case care must be taken to ensure that the image projected is the one that you want to project. There are three aspects to making your promotional material attractive and informative to your customer: style, format, and content.

Style and format

The style and format includes quality of materials used, the use of colour and shape, and the layout of information. It is also how the item is presented and the way in which it actually reaches the customer. For example, a business card produced on thin card on a word processor does not convey professionalism; using an array of different fonts can make text look bitty; an over-worded leaflet or one with text presented in the wrong order will not be read, or its contents not so readily absorbed and understood by the customer.

Just listing the features of a service may no longer be effective in a crowded market-place full of competitors doing the same. Marketing a service for profit needs careful consideration if the right image is to be created to attract and keep the target customers. The 'running order' for information has to be considered carefully in order to take the customer systematically through the advertising message. As with selling verbally, it is important to structure the information to be conveyed in order to lead the customer through to the desired end result.

One tried and tested approach is to use the format, Attention, Interest, Desire, Action (AIDA). Any advertisement has to first catch the prospective customer's attention. Many different devices can be used to achieve this. Because services are intangible it is not possible to show the service itself, only its environment, the tangible equipment or facilities offered, in photographs, cartoons, sketches and drawings. Pictures of 'happy smiling customers' show the outcome of the service. A logo might attract attention if it is already well-known. A challenging or 'newsy' headline can work well. The challenging headline is usually one that asks a question pertinent to the target customer, for example, 'How would your family cope if you had an accident?' for an advertisement promoting accident insurance. The 'newsy' headline must be newsworthy to the target customer and may need to be regularly updated or changed as developments occur within the market and the service provider's business.

It is important to remember that the public buy services to achieve their ultimate benefits, which are based on feelings and emotions, whereas business buy on the basis of cost-effectiveness (see Chapter 3). The attention part of the sales pitch has to have a direct relevance to the target customer's needs, whether those are emotional or 'lifestyle' based, or their need to save or make money. It needs, therefore, to identify a concern, or present the solution to a concern – the ultimate benefit – so that the prospective customer will read on or continue listening to the rest of the message.

It will be realized that, unless the trading name of the business is well known, starting the advertising with the company's name is not really an attention-grabber. At this stage of the format, there is no 'hook' on to which the customer can hang the name; as yet it has no relevance to the reader, viewer, or listener. Nor does it provide a reason for them to read on or continue listening to the message. Starting the message with the business name perhaps speaks volumes that it is more concerned with itself than with the customer; that the customer and the concept of service are not at the start of its business thinking.

The second stage is to create further interest in reading on, backing up the attention already gained. To be succinct, the Attention and Interest parts of the message can sometimes be rolled into one and then perhaps developed in the first part of the body of text. The Interest section is used to re-assure the target customer that the service is right for them, that the service is accredited, proven and popular, and that any fears or resistance they may have are dealt with and allayed.

The third stage is to stimulate desire in the target customer, making them not only want what the service provider is offering, but wanting it only from that source. This section reinforces that the message is aimed at them, personally; that they themselves can now enjoy the benefits of your service. It demonstrates that the offer is 'the natural choice' for them and stresses the main benefit, as well as perhaps a couple of subsidiary benefits to be gained.

Finally, the Action section informs the target customer how to make contact. This becomes the logical position in which to publish the name of the business, together with how the target customer is to make contact. Telephone numbers, e-mail address, Web site details, the address of the business premises if this is to be published (together with directions or a map if necessary), and hours of business are all relevant at this point. Also relevant here are details of how payment can be made and/or how the service can be accessed. Customer comfort can be reinforced with details/logos of any professional or trade bodies to which the business belongs, or accreditations offered.

The style, format, presentation and delivery of the message needs to create an impression, the 'serving suggestion' of what the customer will actually receive. Of course, free pens that break, or do not work, do not convey a message of quality. Incorrect spelling or poor grammar will have the same effect. Unsolicited 'junk' mail, faxes or e-mails are generally unwanted if they have not been targeted to the right type of customer, selectively, and at the right time.

Content

As with style and format, the content of the message should demonstrate that the quality of the customer being targeted is understood, respected, and matched. The advertisement is more likely to be studied if it is written as though to one individual or business, especially as services are a 'people thing'. In this respect, the word 'you' or 'your' should feature prominently, or be implied, in the headline and elsewhere within the body of the advertisement. It is also worth considering whether to match the words and content to the type of customer expected according to the overall market's position within its anticipated life-cycle (see Chapter 4: Strategic direction decisions). Other headline words proven to attract attention are 'new' and 'free'!

Importantly, the content needs to home in on to the main benefit the customer is seeking, readily identifying the service as being the ideal match for their needs. To this end the words, 'which means that' will be stated or implied wherever necessary (see Chapter 3: Features, advantages, benefits – and the ultimate benefit). Summarizing the mission statement into three or four words, or devising a 'strap line' to go alongside the logo can be effective. Such identifying devices can then be reinforced to the customer by appearing on all business stationery, vehicle livery, staff uniforms, equipment, facilities, etc.

Over-worded text might simply be either that which is not clear, concise and to the point, or that which is confusing because it is trying to convey too much information that is not needed at this point. A common mistake made is to try and sell 'off the page', that is, trying to get the advertisement to do the selling. This might be applicable when simply taking orders, that is, when all the customer has to do is decide whether to buy or book their place according to the information presented. Services are a 'people thing' that can often be tailored to individual customer needs. The decision to buy may need to be weighed, not just taken. To maximize sales, this necessitates personal dialogue between the service provider and the prospective customer before the customer has decided whether or not to buy, and which provider to patronize.

Trying to fully describe in print exactly what each customer might gain from patronizing the service can make the text bulky and confusing. It also requires more expensive space to be bought in which to convey it! It becomes vitally important to think through exactly what the advertisement or Web site is there to do. Are prospective customers being invited to make contact so that a dialogue can be opened with them, or is there an attempt at avoiding talking with them? In any case, even facilities sold 'off the page' need to be described in a way that is easy to comprehend, not verbose or cluttered with superfluous detail.

The job of the advertisement or promotional materials promoting a service is to get the target customer to make contact, unless a facility is being offered that might be sold off the page. In either case, however, they will not take any action if there is any perceived risk for them. Understanding potential customers' fears, anticipating them and allaying them, are integral parts of the successful marketing message. Examples of perceived risk, together with possible reassurances, are listed in the tables below:

Table 6.1 *Risks and reassurances*

Risks	Resassurances
Your service will be too expensive:	● Reasonable rates. ● Competitive fees. ● Highly cost-effective. ● Efficient. ● No hidden charges. ● Genuine.
Enquiring about your service will result in a need for immediate commitment or unwanted further attention from you:	● No obligation. ● No salesperson will call. ● Your choice. ● Simply call now for details.
Your service might require too much commitment:	● No obligation. ● No hidden charges, terms or 'small-print'. ● Rights of cancellation. ● Withdrawal terms.
You will be controlling the customer:	● The right for the customer to be listened to and heeded.
Your service will not be competent or reliable:	● Reliable. ● Punctual. ● Right first time. ● Competent. ● Highly trained staff. ● Professional accreditation. ● Guarantee or warranty. ● Customer testimonals.

| Your service will not be timely or will take too long: | ● Punctual.
● Efficient.
● Speedy.
● Prompt.
● Flexible. |
| Your staff may be untrustworthy, brusque or rude: | ● Friendly.
● Caring.
● Professional.
● Genuine.
● Well-trained. |

Businesses looking to hire consultants may face the following fears, in addition to those mentioned above:

Table 6.2 *Consultants: risks and reassurances*

Risks	Reassurances
The consultant might disclose information:	● Confidentiality maintained. ● Confidential service.
The consultant might inaccurately diagnose the problem and waste time:	● Client testimonials. ● Track record. ● Expert. ● Efficient. ● Experienced.
The consultant might upset staff:	● Experienced. ● Diplomatic. ● Professional.
The need for a consultant is an admission, or accusation, of failure on the part of management:	● Professional assistance. ● Advisor. ● Expert. ● Experienced.

Thinking through clearly the purpose of your advertising and then following a structured course, such as the AIDA format described above, helps to identify the form and types of words needed to make up a successful sales message. Remembering that advertising is a form of promise, and that the Advertising Standards Authority establishes guidelines for advertisers, hyperbole is best avoided.

KEY POINTS

- Communications need to convey the right message and the right image to target customers, who need to have them to hand when they are choosing the service provider.
- Any approach to a prospective customer will convey an image of your business.
- You have an image; it is a matter of how you control it.
- The three elements of conveying image in print or by Web site are: style, format, and content. Each must be carefully considered and controlled.
- A tried and tested format for advertising is AIDA – Attention, Interest, Desire, Action.
- Content should include the word 'you' or 'your', at least one main benefit, and points that allay customer fears or feelings of risk.
- The advertising message should be crisp and consistent.

ACTION POINTS

- Check whether the information in your advertising is retained for use by the customer. If not, where do they look up your details?
- Check that your image is controlled correctly and that it is the image you want. If it isn't, change it.
- Is your advertising format well constructed? Do the important parts of it appear in the right sequence?
- Check the consistency of your message.

Putting the business forward as being able to provide a potential solution to its prospective customers' problems can also be achieved in other direct, yet perhaps more subtle, ways than media advertising. Two such ways are: gaining referrals, and networking.

Referrals

Having provided their service for a customer who fits their target profile, many service providers will ask that customer if they would pass on their recommendation to their friends, family, colleagues, business acquaintances, etc. This obviously encourages the word of mouth being sought, yet a more proactive way would be to ask the customer for details of anyone they might be able to refer you to. You can then make the initial contact with that person, not by way of an actual sales pitch, just identifying your business as being available should they wish to contact you at some point in the future. The referral from the first customer provides you with the credibility.

An example of this in practice was used by a new garden service provider to quickly establish his business in his local area. Having found one good customer, he asked if they could refer him on to anyone else, particularly as he was just starting up his business and would appreciate it. He recognized that any referral from his existing customer would probably lead to another good customer. The first customer suggested he might care to call at her aunt's home in the next village. He called at the aunt's house, introduced himself and mentioned her niece's name. He pointed out that he was just on his way home, but if she ever needed any help with her garden then he would be delighted to hear from her. He left her a business card and a leaflet outlining the benefits he could offer. After only two weeks he received a call from the aunt, asking him to quote for some quite extensive garden clearance, replanting and landscaping work. This he did, and was successful in being retained to undertake the whole job and to maintain the garden regularly from then on. The gardener then 'closed the loop' – he went back to call on his first customer and thanked her for the referral. He also gave her some cuttings from plants from his own garden to demonstrate his appreciation.

One can imagine the effect this had on the first customer. Having provided you with a service, when did anyone ever come back to thank you for any referral you gave? The first customer could not help but 'spread the word' about what a nice man their gardener was. Of course the gardener was busy repeating the process, having asked the aunt for the name of someone she could refer him to. Within six months, the gardener's time was fully occupied working for good customers who appreciated him. Leaving 'word of mouth' to chance might have taken six years to achieve the same level of satisfying business.

The above example also demonstrates two important factors in obtaining repeat business or referrals when providing a service. Not only were the service skills provided, to meet and possibly exceed customer expectations, but also the service provider himself was a 'nice man'. It is important to remember that your customer does not know whether (for them) your skills are sufficient until after they have decided to buy. A service is inevitably sold on the image presented by the provider.

Networking

One could say that the gardener described above was networking. He used an existing contact in order to generate more business for himself. Networking is about knowing people already and being recognized by them as possessing the merit to provide the service you are promoting. Networking is the way that a great many service businesses, particularly freelancers, consultants and sole trader service providers, gain the new customers they want.

At first glance, it would imply that the individual person or firm has to know a lot of other people or firms in order to successfully gain new business by networking. Indeed, individuals may be sometimes very well placed in this respect, enabling them to gain as much work as they can accommodate. To market their service for maximum profit however, even those individuals may need to step beyond their existing circle. This might be achieved by forming alliances with other existing networks. Providers of services can become the exclusive, preferred, or recommended service provider for members of trade associations and professional bodies, or the customers of other firms.

An example of a networked alliance is the recommendation by an airline for its passengers to use a particular car-hire firm or hotel at their destination. Likewise, a professional body may have a list of affiliated solicitors or insurance brokers. The dentist might recommend a particular dental health insurance plan, and car manufacturers will recommend their own dealerships for servicing and repairs. In each case there will be some form of financial link or inducement behind the recommendation, but it does feed customers to the service provider. Franchisees of service companies can similarly gain access in their local territory to national contracts arranged by their franchisor: business that they would never have obtained as independent small local providers.

Similar opportunities exist for large and small service providers to link at local level with other businesses, as a strategic part of another firm's business operation. 'Outsourcing' is becoming more the vogue as firms seek ways to reduce overheads and concentrate on their core activities. Office cleaning, catering and security services have been contracted out for many years, and secretaries have been supplied by temping agencies, but now all grades of administrative staff, transport, warehousing, and other previously 'in-house' service activities are being contracted out.

KEY POINTS

- Word of mouth advertising is good, but slow. It can be encouraged by asking for named referrals.
- Referrals are gained from existing satisfied customers to gain more turnover from the type of customer preferred.
- If work arises from a referral, it is important to 'close the loop' by thanking the customer who originated it.
- Networking is about knowing people already and being recognized by them as possessing the merit to provide the service you are promoting.
- Networking can be significantly enhanced by forming alliances with existing networks.
- Networking is the way that a great many service businesses, particularly freelancers, consultants and sole trader service providers, gain the new customers they want.

ACTION POINTS

- Start asking for referrals from your best customers and follow them up.
- Always 'close the loop' for the benefits this can bring.
- Develop a strategy for significantly increasing the size and quality of your network.

Telephone

The telephone is an essential business tool providing a cost-effective means of communication. Because it allows instant personal contact and discussion, the telephone plays an important part in any service provider's business. Yet its effectiveness can be greatly under-utilized because its presence is so often taken for granted. As with crafting interesting and informative advertising copy, care should be taken in how and when calls are made and how they are received. Good training and clearly defined formats in these areas can make all the difference to corporate effectiveness, confidence in the organization, a perception of customer care and the business's bottom line.

The first 30 seconds of any telephone call are crucial, so preparation for them is vital. The opening remarks can be scripted (and often must be), but they must be delivered in words and tone natural to the speaker to retain the personal character of the call. Likewise, it is much more efficient for the key points that are to be discussed to be written down in advance, so that they can be developed and dealt with in a preferred order during the conversation. Preparing for calls in this way enables the conversation to flow with confidence and in a much more positive manner. The mind can concentrate on how the call is being handled instead of struggling to remember what the points are that need to be covered, when perhaps the other person's comments get brushed past or ignored in an eagerness to make comments while they are fresh in the mind. Preparing to make or receive a call also means that all other requisites are to hand, for example, pen, paper, diary, schedules, other internal contact numbers, Web site address, etc.

Professionalism and personality are transmitted down the line, as well as words. In-coming calls should be answered promptly, say by the fourth ring. Both in-coming and out-going calls should be conducted enthusiastically. A friendly and positive tone can be adopted simply by smiling whilst talking and by using the other person's name at least once at a relevant point in the discussion. Listening is an active process. The other person needs to be reassured that their comments are being received and understood, so 'active listening' techniques can be used to good effect on the telephone.

Active listening is a term used to describe the process of making a statement that repeats back to the speaker the essence of what they have just said, or taking time to acknowledge their feelings before allowing the conversation to move on to the next point. Making statements that acknowledge that the existing point or feeling has been understood should precede further questions to the other person. Indeed the other person may not move from the point they are making until they have received confirmation that what they have already said has been understood. Active listening is a powerful communications tool that can be also employed with great effect during face-to-face conversations, discussions and meetings.

When used correctly and with forethought, the telephone can be used in many ways as a primary tool to help market a service for profit:

- to obtain information;
- telecanvassing/teleselling/to make appointments;
- customer enquiries/orders/complaints/customer care.

Obtaining information

A service provider's marketing message can be conveyed whenever it seeks information from others. In this respect it is difficult in some cases to know where research ends and selling begins. Sales for a service provider can sometimes arise from unlikely sources and from previously unconsidered areas of application. To obtain information it is not unusual to be asked to provide information to aid the search. Doing so provides another conduit through which the marketing message can be disseminated.

To obtain information, the question is not so much: 'What do I need to know?' as, 'Who might have the information I need?' When put in these terms, it is obvious that anyone who publicizes their telephone number expects to be phoned; they might also be excellent sources of information or advice. When seeking information or conducting any form of marketing research, we do not always know what it is that we do not know! That is, the ability to gain information can be sometimes best served by keeping an open mind and being aware that not only do we not have the answers, but often we are not aware that the questions exist. Answers to problems often exist outside of the frameworks we construct around problems. The ability to talk with people, telling them what area we are investigating, asking open questions and listening to their answers is one of the best talents a business can have.

Telecanvassing/teleselling/to make appointments

For a great many service providers, telecanvassing is one of the most efficient and cost-effective ways of generating sales enquiries. The instant personal contact can provide the caller with a marked advantage in gaining a decision from the prospective customer. Unfortunately this fact has led to the process being mishandled by many practitioners, either due to lack of experience, lack of training, or as a consequence of poor training. Methods have been taught or copied simply because they work *sometimes*, usually through near-bullying tactics used to pressure the recipient into submission. Results of this is that telecanvassing/teleselling have gained a generally notorious reputation and many people do not like doing it. As a consequence the competition is reduced for those firms that operate ethical telecanvassing and when a system is properly managed with well trained staff, it can yield excellent results.

Understanding a little of the psychology of sales enables the caller to keep control of the conversation in a way that allows the prospect to come more easily to a decision. The first rule is: a prospect will only come to a mutually beneficial decision if he or she is relaxed and comfortable. The words and tone used must maintain this objective and the caller needs to have an empathy for how the recipient is feeling. The prospect must feel that they are in control throughout the call, even though it is actually being led by the caller.

Many telesales calls are not actually trying to sell anything over the phone, they are trying to gain appointments for a representative of the firm to meet the prospect in person. Being pushy or rushing the prospect to a decision too quickly is unlikely to yield lasting results and can do great harm to a firm's reputation, particularly because any service is supposed to be based upon mutual trust and appreciation. To be successful using the telephone to make appointments, the call needs to be thought through and delivered by a well-trained person who can shift with the conversation without losing their course. It is also necessary to remain positive and persuasive, and to be able to deal with objections without being pushy.

Salespeople learn many ways to 'close' a sale; being able to make an appointment to see a specific person or group of people may require the same skills. One technique is to use the 'alternative close' where, whatever the choices made, an appointment is booked. That is, asking when might be the better day for the meeting rather than 'Do you agree that we should meet?' or any other question that could invite a 'No' response. If, for example, Wednesday is chosen, then the 'alternative close' technique can be repeated to help decide whether morning or afternoon would be best, 'So, would the morning, or the afternoon suit you best?' The process can then be repeated again if necessary to determine the actual time of the appointment, 'Would 10 am be suitable, or perhaps 11.30 am?'

The telephone is in a category of its own when the need is to make contact with a specific person. In a commercial situation this person may be 'protected' by a 'gatekeeper', usually a PA or secretary. Their active support is usually necessary for the contact to be made, and often their opinion is counselled. They are not to be patronized, dismissed lightly or pushed aside (although phoning outside of normal office hours often finds the 'boss' still at their desk and probably answering the telephone themselves!).

Selling directly over the telephone is mainly confined to those activities that are 'numbers games'. Selling advertising space in a newspaper or journal; selling time-share apartments or the inevitable double glazing are often badly handled by the caller – and often resented by the recipient – simply because 'numbers games' have impersonal targets and the calls are unsolicited. Once a relationship has been established, calls from salespeople are more likely to be welcomed either for regular orders to be placed, or because they bring special offers to the attention of the recipient. As use of the Internet allows more customers to become better informed and empowered, there may be less need for attempts at selling directly over the telephone.

Customer enquiries/orders/complaints/customer care
Because the telephone offers immediate personal contact, it can be employed with great effect to further customer care; creating, maintaining and improving the relationship between a company and its customers. Help lines are now a common feature of many services, enabling customers to not only make contact with an

organization but to *know* that they have made contact! A customer's opinion of the level of service the company provides will be directly influenced by how they are dealt with on the telephone. All contact with customers comes under the scope of 'customer care' and callers can very quickly change their tone and level of interest within the first 30 seconds of the call.

Enquiries can arise from existing or new customers and must obviously be dealt with courteously, promptly and efficiently by properly trained, competent and confident staff. An enquiry line or help line can send out exactly the wrong signals if it is permanently engaged or always has a long queue of callers waiting to get through. In the right circumstances, automated systems can help in dealing with routine enquiries for information and for routing calls directly to the relevant departments. However, it must be remembered that some callers will want to speak directly with a real, live person and the facility must be capable of achieving this without undue delay. The successful service provider views all calls from customers as being highly valuable, and most definitely not as a nuisance or distraction from other parts of their operation. To charge for such calls, or allow the customer to incur excessive expense when trying to contact the company can show a blatant disregard for customer care. The use of freephone or low cost numbers is certainly an asset that encourages contact from customers who are, above all else, the reason why the company is still in existence.

Specialist training in telephone techniques for all staff is invariably cost-effective, helping the company to market its services at a profit. When a customer query or complaint arises, it invariably has a financial aspect; perhaps a query over a bill, or a complaint about incorrect billing, etc. The root cause of the complaint needs to be identified, since customers who call and who have been delighted by the quality of service they have received are more likely to only query a bill rather than complain about it. The problem may be thus not one of unsatisfactory billing, but one of poor quality of service. If this fundamental point is not picked up immediately, then the call is often routed straight to the accounts department, and from then on the discussion, or argument, centres on the cost instead of on the quality. Accounts people often deal with a great many such complaints and the tragedy is that a great many of them have not been trained in how to deal with them.

Different people have different attributes and inter-personal skills. For example, some people who work in accounts have chosen that career because they prefer the rational 'orderliness' of dealing with figures to the apparent difficulties and problems of dealing with people. Faced with an irate customer who is acting 'irrationally' from feelings and emotions, the rational, logical approach does not get past first base and can often serve to fuel the complaining customer's frustration and anger. Anyone who does not naturally possess the sort of 'people skills' necessary for dealing with complaints will find their job very hard to do in an active service based organization, unless they have the right support and receive positive guidance and tuition in techniques designed to help them cope with this dimension of their job.

Customer care also encompasses positive use of the telephone in initiating calls to customers. Complaints might prompt a written letter of apology rather than a courteous personal call to the customer perhaps preceding the letter, to acknowledge that their complaint has been 'taken on board' and is being dealt with; or that it has resulted in some change to the way the firm now does business. Letters of apology are often originated as an unwelcome but necessary 'damage limitation exercise'. Despite the apology or explanation given, they can appear to be somewhat dismissive and the assumption is that a line can be drawn under the matter. As customers ourselves we are occasionally pleasantly surprised to receive a personal explanation or apology, with real appreciation that someone has taken the trouble to personally see to the matter.

As most households and every business now have a telephone, the power to create excellence in customer care seems somewhat stifled by firms clinging to outmoded systems of communication. The letter has its use, but these days a letter on its own can appear too stuffy and distant, or as a shield behind which faceless management can hide. The impression is often given to the customer that the subject of the complaint has been closed, with or without having made any real impression on the company. Such letters do not allow the company the opportunity to re-open the dialogue with the customer and perhaps snatch victory from the jaws of defeat! An opportunity for being seen to provide real customer care has thus been lost. The very process of initiating a call to a customer in these circumstances demonstrates a concern for that customer and their value to the company.

KEY POINTS

- Because it allows instant personal contact and discussion, the telephone plays an important part in any service provider's business as a cost-effective means of communication.
- Good training and clearly defined formats in the use of the phone can make all the difference to corporate effectiveness, confidence in the organization, a perception of customer care and the business's bottom line.
- The first 30 seconds of any telephone call are crucial, so preparation for them is vital.
- Professionalism and personality are transmitted down the line, as well as words.
- Both in-coming and out-going calls should be conducted enthusiastically. A friendly and positive tone can be adopted simply by smiling whilst talking and by using the other person's name at least once at a relevant point in the discussion.
- Listening is an active process and certain techniques can be used to stimulate and encourage this process.
- The telephone can be used highly constructively for: obtaining information, telecanvassing/teleselling, or to make appointments.
- It can also be used to handle customer enquiries, orders, and complaints.

ACTION POINTS

- Arrange telephone refresher training for all staff.
- Learn the techniques for active listening and arrange courses for all management, as well as staff who come into contact with customers.

INDIRECT MARKETING TACTICS

Indirect methods for promoting a service business are those that are not blatant advertising, yet are designed to attract the target customer without being directly aimed at any one individual or firm. In this context, the methods described below are designed to simply let your prospective customers know that you are there:

● 'word of mouth' advertising/recommendations/testimonials;
● Public Relations (PR);
● writing and publishing a newsletter;
● making speeches and presentations;
● conducting seminars, training courses, master-classes or work-shops.

Word of mouth advertising

This is recognized as being one of the most successful ways for a service to gain new customers. It can also of course work against the service provider if the service does not live up to customer expectations! For the service provider trying to build positively on word of mouth advertising, the problem is that the process inevitably takes a long time, and pre-supposes that the business already has a reasonable number of satisfied customers. Sometimes the snowballing benefits of such commendation arrive too late, after the business has changed hands or ceased trading! Marketing your service for profit means being in control of your business at every stage. That includes helping along the word of mouth advertising whenever possible, making it easy for prospective customers to get in touch with your business by knowing where to find your contact details. Leaving any aspect of your business to fend for itself is the route to unforeseen risk. A way of speeding up the word of mouth process is to ask for referrals, as described earlier in this chapter.

Public relations

The value of good public relations is not confined only to successful marketing since it expands to cover all of a firm's 'publics', and not just those who comprise the firm's target prospective customers. It is a relatively inexpensive way of conveying a message about a business and can have a far greater impact than advertising. Like word of mouth advertising, PR helps to build awareness, which can enhance reputation and credibility, but it can take a long time to become an overnight success! Bearing in mind that success comes from working on the business as well as in it, PR can assist in positioning the business and its services to be attractive to the target customers. The implied endorsement by the media carries weight because people tend to put more faith in firms they have heard about and who are seen to be in the public eye. PR is also a proactive method of defending or helping a business.

Successful PR requires a planned and sustained programme of communications with all the 'stake-holders' of the business who are essential for its success: customers, suppliers, investors, external regulatory bodies, local residents, the community and any opinion formers such as the media or other people in a position to influence the general perception of your business. As mentioned earlier, every business has an image, it is a matter of how that image is controlled. By developing a favourable image, good PR plays an active part in promoting business and, as part of the overall marketing strategy, undoubtedly contributes to higher sales and profits. Prospective customers feel there is less risk attached to approaching the business and existing customers feel no reasons for self-reproach. Staff feel good about working for the business, and recruitment and retention of good staff is made easier. It may even be easier to obtain local planning permission for otherwise contentious expansion.

The type of PR strategy best adopted depends upon three main factors: the area of activity of the business; the competitiveness within the market; and the business's stage of development. The area of activity might be controversial or of itself perhaps create excitement or stimulate interest in a wider audience. Businesses in highly competitive markets require greater promotional activity and PR can markedly influence customers' attempts to differentiate between service providers. Businesses in the early stages of development will have different PR needs from more established ones. Launching a new business, or a new service from an existing firm, or celebrating a notable business anniversary are usually newsworthy in themselves and any such opportunity for favourable publicity should not be missed.

The development of a PR policy is best served as part of the business's overall process of reviewing objectives and determining its planned strategy for achieving them. Since PR affects everyone, each individual within the business will have different experiences of PR problems and much can be gained from consultative discussion about the issues. Employing a professional PR firm is expensive but can be very cost-effective as PR issues are properly handled, monitored and developed.

News releases

Since favourable PR relies heavily upon media coverage, it is important that the needs of the people in the media are understood and maintaining good contacts in the media is a continuous process. Informing the press of a newsworthy event should then be made as easy and straightforward as possible, so that release takes place before the story has gone cold.

What the press wants are stories and genuine news, or interesting background for a feature. They like statistics, especially odd ones, sound bites and provocative quotes, also case studies they can fit a feature around and interesting photographs with a good caption. They like exclusive scoops. Above all, there is immediacy, they want everything now! Even if there is apparently no urgency, it is wise to respond quickly before their priorities change or someone else steals the limelight. News extends to telling people about any aspect of your business that has undergone a change. For example, you are making your service even easier and/or cheaper to access; you are widening the range or scope of your service; or you have recruited new specialist staff, etc.

The press has an insatiable appetite for news, features, events and excitement. It provides opportunities to feed it what it wants, which means that items need to catch the interest of the journalist and editor who is to use it and motivate them to publish in the way that you prefer. Bear in mind the 'house style' of the publication to which you are submitting your news release. Read articles that have been published and model yours specifically for that publication along similar lines, avoiding jargon, flowery language and hype. Pay attention to spelling, punctuation and grammar. Do not underline. Do not put full stops after capital letter abbreviations (for example, DTI). Write out numbers one to ten using letters, and 11, 12, 13, onwards in numerals. Where possible include a professionally produced photograph, preferably taken by the publication's own press photographer. Most newspapers require black and white glossy prints sized 8 × 6 inches or 10 × 8 inches. Colour magazines require 35 mm colour transparencies. A caption describing the 'event' must always be attached to the photograph, along with a contact name, telephone number and address. Of course your business name, logo, and/or telephone number may happen to be in the photograph's background too!

It is important to realize that you have no control whatever over the timing of publication, nor the actual message that is delivered. The press will not carefully reproduce the text and their style may be more cynical. They sometimes get it wrong and there is often no easy way of rectifying the mistakes. Topicality is essential. An advertisement dressed up as PR will be consigned immediately to the bin. A feature must be designed to attract the reader's attention and so needs to be clear, concise, interesting and informative, as well as conveying the desired PR message. A message with a visual content may go to television.

Choosing the right target media is an important part of any successful PR plan. Television can be a two-edged sword and attempts to gain broadcast PR can backfire. For example, using a visit from a celebrity to publicize the business usually results in far more coverage for the celebrity than it does for the business. Just as information submitted in a news release could be published with more cynical intent, television can use your story to feed a totally different message to that which you intended. Unwanted effects on television's large, untargeted and immediate audience can be very hard to remedy. There is a world of difference between crafting a good news release and performing on the spot before the camera, when perhaps only the 'sound-bites' will survive. Interview practice and grooming can make all the difference as the cameras do not concentrate on what is said, more on how and where it is said.

Local press and the free press feature local business stories and often have business sections. The national papers often have specialist business sections. Regional publications, usually monthly or quarterly, and trade publications may be ideally suited as a way to reach sometimes quite specific target customers. Publications such as Willings Press Guide, Benn's Media, and BRAD (British Rate & Data) provide information on all publications in the UK and can be found in most libraries.

News about a company can help a business or damage its reputation. And, even in print, the way that news is presented and deployed can have significant influence on its impact, so it is important to identify the angles that will shape the interpretation of the story and how it will be received by each of the business's target groups. The article is a simplified story about your business, or a particular aspect of it, written from a news point of view.

Headed 'News Release' and indicating when the earliest date the item can be published (usually immediately unless you place on it an 'embargo' until a specified date), it is then necessary to attract attention with a headline, summarizing your news in a few words. There is little point trying to be too clever with the headline as editors will not use it, for fear another newspaper or magazine will use it too. The first part of the news release has to be the 'what?' – what is the story, what has happened? A useful technique is to quote an opinion from someone in 'authority' who can be seen to be endorsing the validity of what you are expressing in the article. Judicious use of dialogue, as though being interviewed yourself, will also keep the reader's attention more than straight blocks of text.

The next part provides some facts and details to flesh out the story, the 'when?', the 'how?', the 'who?' and the 'where?'. (If the story is about your business, mention your geographic location. If the press do not publish your contact details, then at least people know where to ask directory enquiries to find your number.) The question 'why?' usually comes third, along with optional extra material that is relevant to the reader's comprehension and any prices, times, figures or statistics that convey more information about your business. Try to write the article so that it still makes sense if the editor deletes paragraphs from the end. The final part should include your contact number for the benefit of the journalist or editor. You are also trying to get your telephone number and/or e-mail address/ Web site address published for readers to contact your business. The end of the article should be clearly marked 'END' and a note of the word count is useful.

Getting your contact details published can be difficult as the article might then too closely resemble an advertisement. However, if you are offering a free fact sheet or other information for guidance relevant to the reader and that can be tied in with the topic of the article, your details are likely to appear and you have gained your objective. For example, an accountant might provide, 'Ten Top Tips for Reducing Your Tax Bill', or an interior designer might provide a fact sheet headed, 'Secrets of Success: Colour Schemes to Make Your Office More Productive.' The purpose of the fact sheet is to build credibility as well as gain responses. The fact sheet should be kept impartial and its request is not an excuse for unsolicited advertisements in the same envelope. In any event, such material might well be treated as 'junk mail' by its recipient since their attention will be taken up by studying the fact sheet. However, you do now have your prospective customer's details and these can be followed up at the next stage, as part of your selling process, not as PR.

A news release needs to be posted early enough to catch the editorial planning for the edition, at least a week before any publishing deadline. It is wise to chase up your news release to 'check that it arrived' and to find out whether it will be used, or whether they would like more information. Do not be surprised if you have to fax it as well! If it is not going to be used, it is worth trying to find out why to give you pointers for your next attempt.

Bear in mind that journalists can be very busy and sometimes lazy! They respond well when a lot of the work has been done for them and more appears easily accessible if required. They sometimes return to their known sources for further quotes or comment on similar topics at a later date. The more relevant information and/or leads you can give them, the more likely they are to come back to you. If you position yourself to be considered as an expert in your field or local spokesperson for your industry whom they know they can turn to for comment and opinion, this can result in good PR coverage for your business. Local radio and local television news broadcasters often pick up on stories initiated by the local press and may likewise seek a spokesperson or expert for information or opinion.

Non-news or feature articles can be written from a professional or industry stand-point. Such articles can still be seen as newsworthy if they are timely. There may be events happening in the market as a whole that you can comment on, or about which you can express an opinion, indicating to your target audience that you care about their concerns. Changes or events in the wider environment can be used as triggers to get your article published since your information is now 'newsy'. Social, legal, economic, political, or technological changes can all be used as triggers for publication of a suitably relevant article written from the 'human interest' angle. Examples of how such changes have affected your customers and how your service keeps up to date can turn a piece of social commentary into a news release. Case studies and events quoted should be real, not constructed for the purpose. If the item sparks further media interest, the press may want to interview those involved in the story.

Don't turn drama into a crisis
If the business is publicly under attack, a systematic PR policy ensures a response that minimizes damage. In such circumstances staff, investors, suppliers, and regular customers, feel more comfortable about their own positions if they have strong guidance on how to respond to criticism about any unfavourable or controversial aspects of the business. Many service businesses run the risk of something going horribly wrong very publicly – airline, rail or coach crashes, rioting crowds, computer viruses, etc. To avoid turning a catastrophe, or even a crisis, into an unmitigated business disaster, media training is imperative. No Managing Director or spokesperson can be expected to provide a credible interview without practice and professional guidance. Being prepared for calamities is an essential feature of the successful business, and it does not imply that the company spokesperson will appear slick or uncaring. Thinking of what to say to an experienced and accomplished television presenter while walking along the corridor to the TV studio is leaving it too late!

KEY POINTS

- Indirect methods of conveying the marketing message can be highly effective at relatively low cost.
- They aim to attract the target customer without being directly aimed at any one individual or firm.
- Methods of indirect marketing include 'word of mouth' advertising, recommendations, testimonials, Public Relations (PR), writing and publishing a newsletter, making speeches and presentations, and conducting seminars, training courses, master-classes or workshops.
- The value of good public relations is not confined only to successful marketing, since it expands to cover all of a firm's 'publics' and not just those who comprise the firm's target prospective customers.

- It is a relatively inexpensive way of conveying a message about a business and can have a far greater impact than advertising.
- Like word of mouth advertising, PR helps to build awareness, which can enhance reputation and credibility, but it can take a long time to become an overnight success!
- PR is also a proactive method of defending or helping a business.
- Successful PR requires a planned and sustained programme of communications with all the 'stake-holders' of the business.
- The development of a PR policy is best served as part of the business's overall process of reviewing objectives and determining its planned strategy for achieving them.
- Since PR affects everyone, much can be gained from consultative discussion about the issues.
- Employing a professional PR firm is expensive but can be very cost-effective.
- The type of PR strategy best adopted depends upon three main factors: the area of activity of the business; the competitiveness within the market; and the business's stage of development.
- Since favourable PR relies heavily upon media coverage, it is important that the needs of the people in the media are understood, and maintaining good contacts in the media is a continuous process.
- News releases must be newsworthy, properly structured and succinct. The media does not always print what they are given. Mistakes occur. A different story can be interpreted.
- Media training is important for the Managing Director or spokesperson for the company.

ACTION POINTS

- Seriously consider using the services of a professional PR agency.
- Keep a diary of forthcoming public events for development by public relations.
- Undertake a course in media presentation training and practice it.
- Involve all staff in consultative discussions about PR issues.

Letters to the Editor
A letter to the Editor of a local paper, regional magazine, trade journal or even a national daily can produce a positive PR effect, and the author's name, business name and address are usually published at the end of the letter. Excellent PR can be gained by contributing to topical debates in these columns, perhaps through adding your own experience, or turning the debate to provide an alternative viewpoint or show how your service has helped provide a solution for your customers/staff/suppliers. Information or opinion needs to be brief, concise, and to the point, as blatant advertising or waffle will be edited out or leave the letter unpublished altogether. Again, close attention needs to be paid to spelling, grammar and punctuation. The letter can have a title, although the paper may choose to print its own.

Writing and publishing a newsletter
Newsletters can be an excellent way to keep the name of a business in front of its customers, suppliers and staff to retain their loyalty and apparently add value to the relationship. However, producing even a single sheet newsletter that is going to be read and appreciated requires a great deal of planning, commitment, effort, time and money. The newsletter has to compete for attention amongst other unsolicited mail and must, therefore, be seen as being relevant by its target audience. Style, format and tone are important since the newsletter is not dissimilar to a brochure in its job of building credibility and sales. Deciding whether it should be on white or coloured paper, with full colour, part colour, or just black print, glossy or matt, A4, A5 or pocket-book size, with or without pictures, have a serious or light tone, are all decisions that need to be made. Investing in professional writers and photographers can make all the difference to the outcome.

Desktop publishing rarely produces the image needed to reflect the promised quality and reliability required of a public or professional service. If the newsletter is to be an integral part of the PR effort, then professional printing is usually cost-effective, especially for larger quantities. This is not to detract from the benefit of the home-office produced version from the freelance service provider, when a more personal type of correspondence containing information of use to customers might be in keeping. A survey in the United States found that at their first meeting with a customer, 10 per cent of salespeople made a sale; by their fifth contact, 80 per cent had done so. A 'contact' could be a visit, a phone call, a club or society meeting, a Christmas card (or preferably a 'Seasons Greetings' card), or a newsletter. Persistence pays. The newsletter should be produced regularly, say three to four times a year, and sent to everyone with whom the business makes contact. This includes staff, since there should be no distinction between the sales message and the business mission statement. Staff can make excellent ambassadors for the business in their own personal capacities, and services are a 'people thing'.

On the legal front, there are several regulations covering published material and some heavy penalties for not following them. The law of copyright prevents reproduction of text or photographs without the owner's permission. Opinions are not a defence against libel and comparative comment relating to other businesses must be based upon provable facts. It is an offence not to publish the name and address of the printer on the publication. Insurance covering actions for libel, copyright infringement and unintentional misrepresentation is recommended.

Producing a Web site

Web sites are useful for providing and communicating information to visitors quickly and cheaply. As long as the server holding a firm's information is running, customers and potential customers can have access to its marketing message and it can also be used to collect information from them. Even a small firm with a properly set up Web site can, potentially, get the same Internet exposure as a multi-national company. To be successful, Web-based marketing needs to be integrated into the larger marketing plan for the business. Much of the appeal of the Internet is its interactivity, but it should not be used to force advertising on to visitors, such as sending unsolicited e-mails, faxes or mail-shots. To do so can seriously damage a firm's reputation.

Following the ideas suggested under 'Public Relations' above, it is perhaps a better idea for a firm to offer a free fact sheet or some other enticement to be sent to prospective customers. Visitors to the Web site might then leave their postal or e-mail addresses, which can be used later, with their permission, as part of the firm's general marketing database of prospective customers. Part or all of a site can be protected so that only people with a password can access it, so e-mail addresses can be captured when visitors request access to the password. Other, less direct ways, of gaining visibility on the Web is to network with others on a particular topic by joining an appropriate discussion list, or by participating in USENET newsgroups. However, advertising using bulletin boards or newsgroups is frowned upon and not 'netiquette'. Other users of these services are intolerant of any attempt to use this medium for commercial gain.

Listservers allow a firm the ability to build an e-mail contact database automatically from information sent via e-mail or gathered from a form on the Web site. They provide automatic list administration, allowing the firm to send e-mail and other customer communications easily, and can deal with subscriptions and cancellations for services. Listserver subscribers obviously expect to receive a certain amount of information but will stop subscribing if the system is abused by too much 'junk'.

Visitors only return to a site, or recommend it to others, if it is interesting and relevant to them. Ideally, the site offers information that the visitor cannot obtain elsewhere, or enables them to access documents more easily than through the post. The site should be regularly updated and perhaps have added value for the visitor, such as a route for direct e-mail communication with key members of staff, competitions, or special offers such as the free fact sheet idea already mentioned. Even if the site is small, it can include links to lots of other relevant sites. Such hypertext links encourage people to visit the site as a way of finding other useful sites. If this strategy is used, then the links must obviously be placed far enough into the site to show visitors the main part of the company's own marketing message. Collaboration with other Web site hosts reciprocates an increase in traffic.

As with any form of advertising, it is vitally important for a business to decide exactly what the message is to be conveyed. A good site requires interesting copy, good layout, simple graphics and lots of links to related topics. Attention needs to be paid to style, format and content in exactly the same way as for media advertising described earlier. That is, the Web site needs a logical structure, should state clearly the benefits of the service offered and allay any fears the visitor might have about contacting the firm. It is a useful exercise for a firm to study competitors' Web sites and see what they are doing. However a Web site is used, it is of course necessary to publish the Web address in the same way that the company's telephone number and other contact details are published, including the address on all stationery and livery, on answer machines and voicemail messages, and on all advertising and promotional items.

If a Web site is central to the business, a firm can consider running its own Web server. However, it should be noted that running a Web server full time can be very expensive, as most Web sites are not charged on space alone; the greater proportion of the cost is for the bandwidth used, that is the amount of data sent across the Internet. Around a third of the total cost expended can go in setting up the server and Web site, with the rest for maintenance, support and updating. A firm can also incur a substantial penalty from its Internet Service Provider for an excessive number of visitors. Beware too of 'spamming' search engines. This is the practice of registering the site dozens of times with lots of search engines and filling the document with many, irrelevant keywords in order to receive a higher amount of traffic on the site. The practice usually ends up with the perpetrator being removed altogether from search engine lists.

The simplest Web site contains one or two documents held on space leased from a server. Most Internet Service Providers now provide space (typically up to 15 Mb) as part of their standard subscription, and this is more than enough for most small businesses. Third party firms also lease space, often in conjunction with services such as Web site design and management. It may be quite sufficient for a firm to lease space on someone else's server.

Searching the Web using a number of different search engines will locate similar sites and indicate words that need to be prominent for customers to locate a site easily. The site should be 'meta-tagged' (keyworded) appropriately to help various search engines locate the relevant documents within it. Graphics used should strike a balance between attracting attention and holding interest, and enabling the information on the site to be downloaded easily and cheaply. The name given to the Web site should either reflect the type of service on offer or the type of target customer to whom the services are aimed. It must be remembered that a Web site can look very different to visitors depending upon how the site has been designed, encoded, and written, which particular browser visitors are using and how visitors have their own browsers configured. Security for bank or credit card details is still a concern as business transactions over the Internet become more popular. However, much of this worry has been removed by the use of encryption and businesses offering transaction administration services.

Standing up in front of people

Providing services is a 'people thing' and customers cannot assess the quality until after they have committed to paying for them. Therefore, any personal appearance on behalf of a service provider puts a human face to the business and hopefully encourages potential customers to use the service. Standing up in front of people can be a very effective way of delivering a marketing message and gaining the confidence of prospective customers or clients. The occasions when this can be arranged include:

● conducting seminars, training courses, master-classes, or work-shops;
● giving talks, participating in public discussions;
● making speeches and giving presentations;
● presenting trophies and awards.

Of course, some service providers earn their living from running seminars, training courses, master-classes and workshops. However, from the marketing viewpoint, running such events is also a way for the professional expert to gain highly credible publicity for his or her service business before a target audience and the media leading up to it. If the courses are provided free, or at nominal cost, care has to be taken not to give away specific information that customers would otherwise pay more for on a one-to-one consultancy basis, the main point here being to provide a sampler of the firm's expertise. Alternatively, such courses can be profitable in themselves, such that the service provider is in effect being paid whilst advertising the business. This route to gaining publicity and new business whilst earning good returns can be applied with great success by nearly all consultancy firms.

Giving talks or participating in public discussions implies that no payment is received, although expenses may be reimbursed by the host organization. Talks and discussions can of course be undertaken in front of a live audience, by radio or on television. When handled well, these are excellent ways by which a service provider can gain positive publicity. Practice makes perfect and training in presentation skills/media experience is a must if success is to be assured. Even the one-person service provider can gain tremendous free publicity through being invited to give a talk to a local group or share in a broadcast. The actual subject under discussion may be only obliquely related to the service provider's core activity, but if a caring or understanding attitude to the concerns of target customers is shown, then it will be welcomed and appreciated and good public relations will have been achieved.

Making speeches and giving presentations are perhaps more formal ways of achieving similar aims to those described above. They may be conducted before an audience that is not made up of target customers and are generally a more one-sided form of communication. Because of these factors and the fact that there is probably less direct feedback, training and practice by the presenter are absolutely essential. Monologues can be boring when the subject matter is either not directly relevant to the audience or is poorly delivered. Speeches can be used to demonstrate an understanding and care for the 'people' issues, and presentations used to deliver more technical information in an intellectually digestible format.

Presenting trophies and awards can provide an excellent 'media opportunity'; even better when the service provider has sponsored the event or events leading to them. They provide photo and editorial opportunities for either local media coverage or within specialist journals aimed at the service provider's target customers. Many voluntary organizations, sports, social and educational events welcome sponsorship from business, with some only remaining in existence because of it. Presenting the annual trophy to the best student studying in the service provider's field immediately sets the business apart from its competitors and projects an image of excellence for it.

KEY POINTS

- A 'Letter to the Editor' can produce a positive PR effect, and the author's name, business name and address are usually published at the end of the letter.
- Newsletters can be an excellent way to keep the name of a business in front of its customers, suppliers and staff to retain their loyalty and apparently add value to the relationship.
- Producing even a single sheet newsletter that is going to be read and appreciated requires a great deal of planning, commitment, effort, time and money.
- There are legal issues governing the publication of newsletters.
- Web sites are useful for providing and communicating information to visitors quickly and cheaply.
- Even a small firm with a properly set up Web site can, potentially, get the same Internet exposure as a multi-national company.
- A Web site should be integrated into the company's overall marketing strategy and should contain information that they could not get elsewhere, except perhaps by post (Annual Reports, etc).
- Collaboration and Web site links with other firms increase traffic to each of the sites.
- It is useful to keep an eye on competitors' Web sites.
- Web sites should not be so clever that their information cannot be downloaded by a visitor.
- Running your own commercial Web site can be expensive; leasing should be considered.
- The Web site address should be relevant either to the company name or to its target customers.
- Standing up in front of people can be a very cost-effective way of disseminating knowledge of your business to target audiences. Examples are: conducting seminars, training courses, master-classes, or workshops, giving talks, participating in public discussions, making speeches and giving presentations, or presenting trophies and awards.

ACTION POINTS

- Consider all the possible avenues through which the marketing message can be disseminated.
- Develop a strategy for using a selection of them.
- Employ the Web site as an active marketing tool, integrated within the overall marketing strategy.
- Click on competitors' Web sites yourself. Make notes.
- Write Letters to the Editor on any topical issues that will achieve positive PR.

7

Managing the process

'It is wiser to build fences at the top of the cliff, rather than having strategies for rushing ambulances to the bottom.'

The very nature and essence of services mean that pricing can often be quite fluid. Service providers more often than not do not have a price or fee, rather they have a way of calculating their price or fee. In many cases, successfully applying negotiating and selling skills can make all the difference when the objectives are to gain optimum profit from supplying a service and ensure that due payment is received on time.

As described in Chapter 5, a definitive 'going rate' is sometimes much harder to establish for a service than it is for the price of tangible goods or simple access to facilities. The price of an intangible service might be indicated by the service provider, but its value is decided by the customer. For many services, the participation of the customer before, during, and possibly after the transaction allows them the opportunity to negotiate. Coupling this with their involvement in perhaps tailoring the service to their needs, means that they will also want the right to tailor the price they pay. The decision to buy a service may be more often weighed rather than just taken.

While Chapter 5 discussed many of the variable elements to be considered in pricing a service for profit, this chapter suggests some techniques for achieving success in negotiating the service contract and advice on ensuring that due payment is forthcoming. Other books possibly explore these topics in more depth than is available here, but the real skills necessary can only be gained by practice and through personal experience.

NEGOTIATING

The service provider should avoid giving anything away for free or at low cost up front. Often the only thing a service provider has to offer is their time, facilities, or their knowledge. Once one of these have been given for free, the customer may have no further need for them. Particularly when the customer is larger than the service provider, a request can be made for a 'sample' of the service. This should be avoided and perhaps countered by negotiating the terms of the trial run according to your normal terms and conditions, which might then be modified in light of a valuable contract.

Before negotiations commence with a prospective customer, there are three main questions to be considered that may determine whether the negotiation should proceed:

1. Does the customer have the means by which to pay for the service? It would not be considered unreasonable to ask this question in a diplomatic way. For example, an enquiry can be made whether a particular budget number needs to be referenced on the bill or invoice, whether payment is being recovered through an insurance claim, or some form of grant, etc.

2. Does the person negotiating on behalf of the customer have authority to do so? If they do not then the negotiation cannot be finalized and might be better adjourned until the person with authority can be present. A commercial customer may well be able to quote an order number against which the service is to be booked.

3. Does the customer have the need for the service? Some customers engage in 'fishing expeditions' just to discover what information they can glean about markets and competitors, or to try and obtain valuable technical information and solutions to their problems from the unwary expert. Once a service has been provided, it is no longer needed.

Negotiations can be competitive or collaborative. Negotiations are competitive if one party wants to 'win', since this also implies that the other party must 'lose'. The result of this can be confrontation; and if one party 'wins' at the other's expense, this may jeopardize further business opportunities. It is assumed here that negotiations to be considered will be primarily where neither party wants a win/lose or lose/lose outcome.

In collaborative negotiation the objective is to strive for a 'win/win' result, with each party obtaining the best possible deal without creating unnecessary conflict. Such negotiations are, therefore, both collaborative and constructive events. Rather like slicing a cake, the objective is not to gain more cake than the other party. Negotiating a contract or deal might be described as the process of agreeing how the cake is to be sliced so that each party gets most of the part of the cake that it prefers. The objective is thus more easily obtained when the two parties prefer different parts of the cake, and is made more difficult when both parties want the same part of the cake! The result however should be an agreement that is satisfactory to both parties, that is, one that maximizes mutual advantage.

There is no definitive way to negotiate and each person develops a style that suits them as their negotiating skills improve with practice. However, there are five essential stages in the negotiating process, which should be recognized and understood:

● preparing;
● discussing;
● proposing;
● bargaining;
● agreeing.

Preparing

Preparation is essential if negotiation is to be successful. There are two main areas of preparation required: first, define your objectives and rank them in order of priority and, second, research the subject and check whether any apparent constraints are valid.

Define your objectives
Decide in advance what a positive outcome should contain for
you. Such objectives should be specific, measurable, realistic and
achievable. In other words, you should have a clear idea of what
you want from the other party. It is wise to write down the objectives and to do so in their order of priority, in categories of:

1. must achieve;
2. intend to achieve;
3. like to achieve.

Similar preparation and forethought should be given to how far
you are prepared to go in concessions; deciding which parts you
are not willing to give up, which you would prefer not to concede,
and those which you are quite flexible about. For example, all the
negotiable aspects of providing your service need to be listed in
readiness for a meeting with a potential customer or client.

Research
Gather as much information as possible about the subject to be
negotiated, any assumptions that have been made and any
possible constraints that appear at first glance to restrict the negotiation. Try to think and research 'outside the box'. Before entering
negotiation with a prospective customer, try to establish a starting
price that is realistic to them by considering what their deadlines
are and what the cost is to them of not availing of your service.
This must then be balanced with an awareness of the range and
availability of competitors. The person with the most information
is usually the one who does better in negotiations.

Discussing

This is the process of exploring each other's needs (finding out
which part of the cake they prefer!). It may involve making tenta-
tive opening offers, which must be realistic if there is to be scope
for a satisfactory conclusion. If both parties are cooperative and
prepared to collaborate for an agreement, then progress can be
made. If one party is competitive then difficulties will arise. To get
round this, suggest that at this stage you just wish to talk about the
subject matter and cover the main issues that are at stake for each

party, allowing the discussion to then develop naturally. By establishing more of a relationship with the other party, asking questions to find out more about their needs, the chances of finding a mutual agreement is increased.

Proposing

This is the stage where proposals are given and received by both sides. It is important to trade rather than concede. Word your proposals as, 'If you... (give me something), then I... (will give you something)'. There is no power in saying, If I/Will you? For example, saying, 'If you can provide the facilities, then my costs are lowered and I can reduce my price' sounds much stronger than, 'If I lower my price, then will you provide the facilities?' Note also that a valid reason was given for you to be able to negotiate price – a drop in price should never be given away. Commercial customers seek only three things: to save money, to make money, or to transfer risk. Negotiation about money should, therefore, centre on cost-effectiveness, not price. The cost-effectiveness stance can likewise be employed with non-commercial customers by stressing the benefits the service provides and its timeliness.

Following this line, if concession has to be made it would be better to concede something of variable value; something that does not cost you much but that is seen as valuable by the other party. For example, a consultant who can only sell his or her time might offer to add an extra day or so on to a contract for free, or not charge for all of the days worked. Such an offer does not actually cost the consultant much, but would otherwise cost the client many hundreds of pounds. (NB free days are counted at the end of a contract, not at the beginning.) Likewise, a contractor can offer to include an extra duty that would otherwise cost the customer more money. The reason this sort of proposal is to be preferred is that it preserves the integrity of the normal fee rate. Often the other party's prime reason for wanting to negotiate is to be able to report back that they had achieved a better than standard deal.

Bargaining

After discussing each other's requirements and exchanging

information, the proposals are made and bargaining starts. Sometimes these two sections become almost indistinguishable and bargaining may arise before proposals are suggested. Choosing your words carefully is important here, as it was in phrasing the proposal. The word 'normal' or 'usual' can be applied in answer to the questions, 'What do you charge?' or, 'How long will it take?' etc. 'My normal fee is £x' allows room for negotiation without actually shifting position. 'This service usually takes z days' allows room for exceeding customer expectations or not allowing any discount if their deadline is earlier. Generally speaking, you receive more if you start off asking for more, or will concede less if you start off offering less. If the customer baulks at your 'normal' fee, price, time, etc, the way has been left open for negotiation. Proposals and bargaining can remind one of watching a tennis rally as the ball is sent back and forth across the net. Words such as 'about' and 'approximately' should not be used since these will invariably be picked up on by a skilled negotiator and used to increase concessions from you.

Price and/or level of service to be provided are not the only subjects for negotiation. Terms and conditions of a contract must be agreed, particularly concerning how and when payment is to be made and received. Agreement needs to be reached about sundry payments such as expenses, travel, etc. Any insurance covers that might be needed should be clarified to establish which party is responsible for any claims that might arise. Any facilities to be used need to be agreed, and the time frames worked out as far as possible. The benefit of spending time in preparation and forethought on these issues is realized here.

Agreement

When agreement is being reached and the negotiation shows signs of drawing to a close, attempts should be made to finish swiftly without reverting again to the bargaining stage. It is time to summarize what has been discussed and agreed. If the other party does not confirm their position or offer in writing, then you can write to them thanking them for their time and confirming the details of the agreement. If a dispute arises later on, such a letter will be invaluable as the main reference document.

KEY POINTS

- The characteristics of services mean that pricing can often be fluid and service providers may not have a set price but a way of calculating their price.
- The value of a service is decided by the customer.
- Customers will want the right to negotiate the price of a service, perhaps more than they would for the supply of goods.
- All a service provider has to offer is their time, facility or knowledge. If these are given free, the customer may have no need to pay for more.
- The customer must have the means to pay.
- The customer must have the authority to pay.
- The customer must have the need to pay.
- Negotiations can be competitive or collaborative.
- Collaborative negotiations seek a win/win result.
- There are five main steps in negotiating: preparing, discussing, proposing, bargaining, agreeing.
- Preparing means defining objectives and carrying out research.
- Discussing may involve making opening offers, exploring the ground.
- Proposing means saying 'If you…, then I…'
- Bargaining covers the details.
- Agreeing means summing up and confirming in writing.

ACTION POINTS

- Decide the basis for your pricing strategy.
- Estimate the value of your service through the eyes of your customer; what is their cost of not using the service?
- Avoid giving away free service before the customer has paid for any.
- Always check that the customer can pay, will pay and needs to pay.
- Seek win/win solutions.
- Go on a negotiating skills course and practise, practise, practise!
- Always follow up agreements in writing to avert problems later on.

GETTING PAID

Some services can be destined to collapse for the want of cash, no matter how profitable the service is. The problem arises when cash payments have to be made out of the business before revenue due from its invoices can be obtained. For example, a service firm supplying temporary staff to customer organizations usually has to pay the 'temps' wages weekly or fortnightly, whereas its invoices to customers may only be accepted on a monthly basis. This means that the faster the firm grows, the more working capital it needs just to continue in existence. A sort of 'black hole' for cash is spawned and the business will rapidly disappear into it unless a suitable strategy is adopted to prevent this from happening. One such solution might be the use of factoring or invoice discounting to supply cash on a more immediate basis. This can be at least as expensive as an overdraft, but does have the advantage of a more stable financial footing.

Whether a service provider gets paid, and when, has to be determined well before the service is provided. Even cash businesses suffer from bad debts and invoicing customers carries even higher chances of late payment or non-payment. It is estimated that eight out of ten bad debts are from people who never intended to pay in the first place. This may or may not be because of criminal intent since a lack of budgeting on their part or opportunism can have the same result. Running throughout the service provider's dealings with a customer is the concept of relationship. This means that measures should be taken to ensure payment that do not obstruct the relationship or bring it lightly into conflict. There are three main stages where 'fences can be built at the top of the cliff' rather than having to 'rush ambulances to the bottom'. These are:

- before undertaking any service contract;
- during/immediately after the contract;
- after due time has elapsed.

Before undertaking any service contract

The first defence is to establish the terms and conditions under which the service will be provided. In business contracts, 30 days may be normal but this is not cast in stone. Payment, part-payment or a deposit can be requested in advance, or invoiced daily, weekly, fortnightly or at the end of each stage in a contract, depending upon the type of service rendered and the custom and practice accepted for that type of service. Whatever terms are decided upon, the customer must be clearly aware of them before a contract commences. It is not acceptable in law for a supplier to simply present terms on the back of the invoice, when the service has already been provided. It may be agreed that the customer's normal payment terms will apply, in which case any consequences of this must be considered.

A second defence for the service supplier is to check the credentials of the customer, if possible by finding out what sort of reputation they have amongst other service providers. Alternatively credit references can be sought from commercial credit referencing agencies or from the customer by way of trade references. The service provider may decide to have different credit policies for different customers, to reflect the level of risk involved for their business. It is necessary to consider the ability of the business to withstand the debt not being paid, or the consequences of payment being delayed. Obviously a business should think very seriously about extending further credit if it has experienced any difficulty over previous payment from the customer.

Thirdly, having a professional image and reputation and providing a quality service all help the customer to value the business relationship, making a bad debt or late payment less likely. A common reason adopted by customers to justify late payment or no-payment is that the service provided was slow, late or not of the standard required.

Fourthly, the company must take care not to 'put all its eggs in one basket'. Over-dependence on only one customer has led to the ruin of many service providers when their major customer has folded, merged, been acquired, or dropped them.

During/immediately after the contract

The first defence at this stage is for the service provider to gain clarification that payment will be forthcoming as agreed. Obtaining an order number from a commercial customer shows that authority for the expenditure has been sanctioned. An authorized signature should be obtained as soon as the service has been provided, confirming that all was in order. This document may take the form of a job card, delivery note or satisfaction note. Documents sent through the post should have an acknowledgement sheet on top for the customer to sign and fax back or send back to acknowledge safe receipt of the items.

The bill or invoice must be properly and accurately made out – mistakes can be used by customers as an excuse to delay payment or can genuinely cause difficulties that delay payment. Likewise, the right person must receive the bill or invoice otherwise it will be 'lost'. Knowing how and when customers normally pay their bills helps to avoid missing an end-of-month or similar deadline for an invoice. For the smaller service provider or one suffering cash flow problems themselves, knowing a customer's routine takes some of the stress out of waiting for payment. It also enables any unusual delays in payment to be spotted and queried.

For the smaller service provider, a telephone link with staff in the accounts department of a larger business customer can provide a way of checking that their payment is being processed. The smaller service provider or contractor providing services for a larger firm can often feel at a marked disadvantage, indeed at the mercy of the larger firm. Not knowing when payment might be received can place undue stress on the small business; the ability to make a simple telephone call without 'rocking the boat' can help to alleviate this stress. If the relationship is good, then a quick call can check that the invoice was received, or to query why payment has not been received even one day beyond the normal time allowed in the firm's terms and conditions. This is better than waiting for, say, a further month to elapse before sending a second statement and simply living in hope!

The large company might use the telephone to prompt payment from individual customers, although this usually occurs only when a written reminder has not been acknowledged and the account remains outstanding. Again, having a professional image and proven reputation for providing a quality service helps the customer to value the business relationship and be more likely to pay on time.

After due time has elapsed

The service provider must chase early, and keep chasing. When debtors exceed their payment deadline, paperwork has to be generated in case the amount owed becomes a bad debt and proof of this is necessary for the company's Inland Revenue and VAT returns. Statements must be issued, which would not have been raised had the amount been paid. All this paperwork must be accurate and correct in every detail, or again the less scrupulous customer can use it as a delaying tactic.

If the debtor shows no sign of paying, the business must consider its response. Legal remedies are available through the County Court, perhaps as a Small Claim if the amount in question is for less than £3,000. Taking a claim to the Small Claims Court results in the issue of a County Court Summons for payment unless a valid defence is accepted. There is no guarantee of payment, but the company does have the satisfaction of a County Court Judgement (CCJ) in its favour and many debtors will prefer to pay before reaching this stage rather than incur the effect that a CCJ will have on their credit rating.

KEY POINTS

- Suitable funding arrangements may be necessary, for example, factoring.
- It is estimated that eight out of ten bad debts are from people who never intended paying in the first place.
- The concept of relationship runs through all dealings with the customer.
- Create fences before, during and after a contract to prevent bad debts from arising.
- Ensure that all paperwork is meticulously accurate and timely.
- Legal remedies should only be sought as a last resort, but should not be shied away from.

ACTION POINTS

- Examine your company's credit control system.
- Find ways of improving both cash flow and customer care through better debtor management.
- Create the fences necessary to stop customers falling into debt.
- Ensure that your service is always professionally delivered and that paperwork is meticulous.

MANAGING SERVICES AND FACILITIES

A distinction was drawn at the beginning of this book between supplying services and providing facilities, although in current received wisdom any business not making or supplying goods is seen as a being a service. It has been suggested earlier that supplying services inherently involves providing the customer with the attention of people to deal with their needs, whilst facility providers allow customers to use their premises, equipment or systems for a fee. Many business, ranging from airlines to restaurants, offer both personal service and the use of facilities in one package.

However, if a differentiation can be made between these components, then the relative priorities of management will be different between services and facilities, as well as being markedly different from the skills required to manage the production and supply of goods. The management of face to face or telephone encounters with live 'real-time' customers calls for very different skills and experience to the management and staffing of technical machinery and equipment. The management of services generally requires a facilitating approach, rather than one that is overly controlling.

The question arises as to who, or what, is at the sharp end of satisfying the customer at any particular point in time. For a service, everything depends upon the person in front of the customer. Like the needle in a vinyl record player is responsible for high quality transmission of all the resource of the system behind it, then front-line service staff are responsible for imparting to the customer all the energy, enthusiasm, power, resources and customer care of the company. No matter what cost has gone into the system, it can come to nought if staff are not well supported, well trained, well managed, or well rewarded. Using a facility, the customer looks for the quality to be provided in the fabric of the environment and efficiency of the equipment. Both services and facilities operate in 'real-time' since their purchase or use by the customer is transient.

The cost bases of services and facilities are different. The former may involve very little outlay on capital items and have specific insurance requirements, whereas the latter requires more significant capital outlay and different insurance requirements. Investment in services will be embodied in the staff, whereas investment in facilities is targeted towards keeping equipment up to date and well maintained. These are important points to consider when considering any marketing plan or strategy for profit since the definition of who or what is at the sharp end determines how the benefits of being a customer are to be described and implemented.

Managing a Web site

A Web site should be registered with all of the major search engines. To check where their site is registered, a company can enter its own site address into www.did-it.com for the information. Information contained on a Web site should be updated regularly, as should any links it contains to other sites. It is advisable to aim for a general change of content every three months to keep the site interesting and encourage repeat visits. Care has to be taken not to infringe other people's copyright by using graphics, photographs or text without their written permission.

It is useful to know how many visits are received by the site and while basic counters can record the number of 'hits' there have been, it is also useful to know how long visitors stayed, which links they used the most, etc. This information can provide useful data for sales and market research purposes. It must also be remembered that a successful site can generate a lot of feedback from visitors in the form of e-mail messages, so strategies for dealing with these need to be prepared in advance. Managing a Web site can become almost a job in its own right, since the site itself becomes almost a service in its own right. All information published on the site should be subject to the company's existing corporate standards and checked for accuracy, style and content and all links should be checked to make sure they operate perfectly.

DEFINING THE MISSION

At its simplest, a mission is a statement of purpose guides the activities of the business. It is a summary of 'what the business does'. A mission statement embodies the core values of the business and should be understood by all staff, customers, financial investors and suppliers. It provides the guiding direction for developing policy and strategy, seeking out and recognizing opportunities, and making resource allocation choices and decisions. Service companies often find it easy to seek and take on work outside their main activities without thinking whether they should. Apparent opportunities can be measured against the aims of the company set out in the predetermined mission statement, preventing the company from being diverted from its chosen path, or ratifying a decision to pursue the opportunity. Fundamentally, a mission statement answers the question, 'What business are we in?'

Vision and strategic objectives

Vision and strategic objectives drive the business forward to its long term aims. They are statements describing where the company sees the ultimate goal posts and the challenging but achievable targets along the way. They state the company's desired competitive position within the likely future environment. Strategic objectives spell out the targets in more detail for the short and medium term and will probably cover marketing, finance, staff development, quality, etc. They may also include diversification, mergers, acquisitions, joint ventures or other strategic alliances.

ASSESSING RESOURCES: TIME, PEOPLE, CASH, FACILITIES

Management for profit can be described as the process of achieving optimum goals through the efficient use of scarce resources. Marketing a service for profit similarly requires a realistic assessment of the time, people, cash and facilities available in order to meet viable demands of the business. The Marketing Audit described in Chapter 8 enables management to take stock of these factors as well as providing the basis for assessing the firm's position as a marketing based company. Emphasis has been placed throughout this book on the importance of people in the organization and that providing a service is essentially a 'people thing' that takes place transiently. Time, and the ability to 'get it right first time' are, therefore, of the essence, requiring the right people trained and equipped to do the right things in the right place at the right time.

KEY POINTS

- Although sharing common characteristics, management priorities can be different for services and facilities.
- Management of services requires a facilitating style, whereas facilities require a more controlling approach.
- The successful company invests in the 'who' or 'what' that is ultimately in front of the customer.
- The cost bases of services and facilities are very different from each other and thus the marketing style needs to be different.
- Web sites need to be well managed, registered with all major search engines and checked for accuracy and technical efficiency. Care must be taken not to infringe other people's copyright.
- Web sites can be a useful source of marketing and sales research data.
- A mission statement is a useful tool for stating what the business does and for keeping it on that track.
- A vision statement and strategic objectives drive the business forward towards its long term goals through targets set along the way.
- The business must have a realistic register of it resources – time, cash, people, facilities.
- Services are transient and need to be got right first time. People are the key.

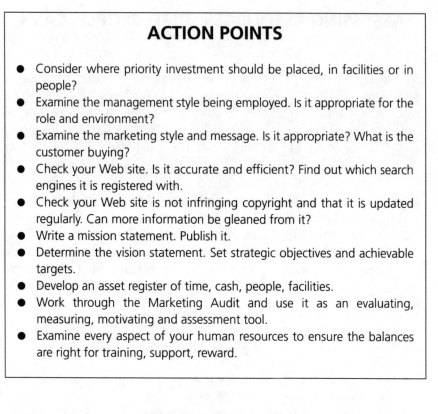

ACTION POINTS

- Consider where priority investment should be placed, in facilities or in people?
- Examine the management style being employed. Is it appropriate for the role and environment?
- Examine the marketing style and message. Is it appropriate? What is the customer buying?
- Check your Web site. Is it accurate and efficient? Find out which search engines it is registered with.
- Check your Web site is not infringing copyright and that it is updated regularly. Can more information be gleaned from it?
- Write a mission statement. Publish it.
- Determine the vision statement. Set strategic objectives and achievable targets.
- Develop an asset register of time, cash, people, facilities.
- Work through the Marketing Audit and use it as an evaluating, measuring, motivating and assessment tool.
- Examine every aspect of your human resources to ensure the balances are right for training, support, reward.

CUSTOMER CARE

In today's highly competitive markets, customers are better informed, better equipped, and willing and able to travel in order to get what they want. Often the only distinguishing factor between one service provider and another is the perceived level of customer care received by the buyer. Local firms will lose out if a more distant company is seen to provide a better package of service, and the Internet is extending choice globally. Likewise the large national organization can lose out to local service providers who can perhaps provide more personal service to discerning customers. Customer care lies at the heart of marketing a service for profit.

Previous chapters have indicated that the quality of a service is only that which can be described by customers. A customer's opinion of the level of service the company provides will be directly influenced by how they are dealt with as a person. All contact with customers comes under the scope of 'customer care' and customers can change their opinion of a firm very quickly, for good or ill. For a service based company, every member of staff has a role to play in customer care, such that it is at the core of the company's identity, culture and philosophy. A succinct vision statement and accompanying clearly defined, concise, mission statement should embody the message of customer care.

Managers need to ensure that their own customer care skills are up to the mark before they can expect to see any improvements from their staff. Training, guidance and support are needed by anyone in the 'front-line' of a business to ensure that the values enshrined in the company's policies are adhered to and implemented in the spirit in which they were written down. The successful company has laid down specific procedures to guide staff in their routine tasks, such as answering a telephone within four rings, returning calls within two hours when a return call has been promised, or opening a further service counter when more than four customers are waiting for service.

Customer areas should be kept accessible, clean and safe, with facilities provided for any problems that might arise. Best results can often be gained by allowing staff to draw up their own customer care procedures and then discussing them in a constructive quality forum supervised by management. Handled positively, this can bring out some excellent ideas for enhancing customer care, often at minimal cost, and helps to ensure staff 'ownership' of the ideas and, therefore, their consistent application.

Good customer care is driven both by behavioural actions and attitudinal actions. The behaviour of a member of staff can be controlled by company rules; their attitude can only be governed by themselves. The company can selectively employ applicants who exhibit the desired attitude and then train them in the required behaviours. Changing existing staff attitudes can usually only be achieved through discussion and exploration of the routes that will allow such change to be accommodated by the individual. Role-playing and transactional analysis might then be used to teach awareness of the benefits of adopting a preferred attitude. A person's attitude is often exhibited involuntarily by them to others, with body language such as posture, involuntary gestures, facial expressions and other non-verbal communication speaking volumes to the customer. In many services, eye-contact with the customer is essential to establish the relationship, yet a member of staff may be too shy to do this and it is construed that they are either bored or lying.

Management can react to the actions of their staff in only one of three ways: by criticism, praise, or ignoring them. Criticism tends to be the most common vocal response, picking up on inappropriate or wrong behaviour. It may or may not be followed by constructive training in the preferred behaviour. Praise goes a long way towards reinforcing preferred behaviour and is a powerful tool in developing customer care attitudes. Unfortunately, most of the time the actions of staff are simply ignored by management. This has the result of reinforcing unwanted behaviour, allowing negative attitudes to persist and not recognizing merit when it is deserved. Ignoring how staff accomplish their routine tasks also makes it very difficult to demand later a change in either behaviour or attitude.

Companies may likewise ignore the good intentions of customers. Most service companies say that they welcome comments and suggestions from customers on how the service might be improved. Whilst there may be a communication channel established for receiving such constructive comments, very few companies appear to have established systems for feedback on how such comments have been received by higher management. Often the signals sent out by a company are that it is so big that it will only force itself to bother with complaining customers, while the customer offering advice or comment can be virtually ignored. Surely the customer who takes the time and trouble to offer what they see as constructive suggestions is demonstrating a desire for loyalty, both ways.

As many service providers are aware of the need to create customer loyalty for survival in their highly competitive markets, it seems strange that developing feedback systems for providing more personal responses are not given priority. Perhaps the assumption is that, whilst comments will inevitably arise from individual customers, the company can only respond en masse, if at all. Yet a simple telephone call to the customer from higher management can have a dramatic positive effect on the customer's perception of the firm and its devotion to customer care. The higher management are no longer faceless people hiding behind their important job titles, but real people with a passion for quality.

KEY POINTS

- Often the only distinguishing factor between competing service providers is the level of customer care they achieve.
- Excellence in customer care lies at the heart of marketing a service for profit.
- Customer care centres on treating each customer as an individual.
- Every member of a service company is involved in customer care.
- Managers' own customer care skills must be up to the mark.
- Specific pointers can be laid down for routine aspects of the business to achieve simple elements of customer care.
- Good customer care is driven by both behavioural and attitudinal factors of the staff and management.
- Management can react to staff actions in one of three ways: criticism, praise, or ignoring.
- Each has its own implications for customer care.
- Companies often miss wonderful opportunities to improve their customer care by ignoring messages from customers and staff.
- Often excellence in customer care is only a phone call away.

ACTION POINTS

- Is customer care really at the heart of your operations? Try phoning up with a constructive suggestion. Track it through your systems.
- Phone your help-line or customer service line. Check it out.
- Create a customer care culture.
- Have customer care written into all job specifications and job profiles.
- Arrange for customer care workshops for all management.
- Arrange for team building courses for managers.
- Discuss attitudes with staff (and management if necessary!).
- Arrange for customer care workshops for all staff.
- Phone a customer who recently made contact with the company. Make notes. Take action.

DEALING WITH CUSTOMER COMPLAINTS

Chapter 6 described how positive use of the telephone can be made to convey the marketing message through help lines and customer service numbers, and this included aspects of dealing with customer complaints. In essence, the successful service provider views all contact from customers as being highly valuable, and most definitely not as a nuisance or distraction to be sidelined from other parts of their operation. If management's objective is to undertake only a 'damage limitation exercise' in response to complaints, an opportunity for being seen to provide real customer care has been seriously missed.

Faced with customer dissatisfaction or complaint, it is essential that the customer's feelings are acknowledged and addressed first. This means first listening to the customer without interruption and then demonstrating empathy without patronizing; agreeing in a low, calm voice, that if the complaint is justified then the customer's feelings are also justified and that the customer certainly deserves an apology for the company having made them feel that way. If this is not done, then the matter cannot be resolved without the customer's negative feelings towards the company remaining and probably a very public battle then ensuing for 'justice'. Taking a defensive stance should be avoided so as not to allow 'battle-lines' to be drawn, and just letting the customer run out of steam, hoping they will 'calm down and see reason', may exhaust the customer to a point of exasperation.

Only when the customer feels that they have succeeded in gaining recognition and understanding of their feelings of disappointment, frustration or anger, will they start to let go of those feelings, acknowledge that an apology for their upset is being offered, and start to consider possible ways of resolving their complaint. If the complaint is being made face to face and other customers are listening, it is only at this point that the complainant might allow themselves to be taken aside for the matter to be properly discussed and resolved in a calm and practical manner. The process described above must still be carried out even if the customer is not exhibiting any of the feelings mentioned; the first objective being to show that the service provider cares.

Having acknowledged the customer's feelings, it is then necessary to confirm the facts with the customer, perhaps by asking the customer to repeat them and, if necessary and convenient, taking written notes. The root cause of the complaint then needs to be identified and defined. Occasionally, the problem may not be as it appears to be on the surface, for example, a complaint might not be about unsatisfactory or incorrect billing, but really one to do with having received poor quality of service. This can easily occur if there is a standard charge for the service and the service did not appear to warrant the cost. If this fundamental point is not picked up immediately then the symptom may be efficiently dealt with, but the problem left unrecognized and unresolved.

A very important step is to ask the customer how they would like the situation to be remedied. Trying to force a standard 'remedy' on to every diverse complainant rather detracts from the idea of treating the customer as an individual. Sometimes all the customer really wants is a sincere apology. Of course a refund or other compensation must be offered in all cases, and the service provider should have laid down policies that enable complaints to be dealt with quickly and efficiently on the spot. If a complaint does need to be referred to higher management, then that needs to be explained to the customer, along with the reasons why their complaint needs to be referred upwards. One such reason might be that all *unusual* complaints have to be brought to the attention of senior management. (NB all complaints are *serious* to the customer or they would not have bothered to complain.) The process that is to follow should be described to the customer and agreement reached that it is acceptable to them.

Passing a complaint 'sideways' to another department should only be allowed by a supervisor or manager, who should themselves refer the matter to the relevant department. The customer should not be expected to have to go to further inconvenience or in any way allowed to feel they are being given the 'run around'. Lengthy or bureaucratic procedures carried out in the customer's presence but designed more to satisfy internal administrative policies will only serve to dramatically increase customer dissatisfaction.

If the complaint has been referred, then it is clearly the job of the manager who referred it to follow it up and ensure that it is being dealt with. Irrespective of how long the complaint does take to be settled, it is vital that the customer is contacted again within a matter of days, preferably by the manager to whom they were referred. This reassures the customer that their complaint has indeed been taken on board by the company, whether or not it has yet been resolved. Customers do not like to feel they are being ignored or that their complaint has been side-lined. A vital ingredient of 'customer care' is demonstrating that the individual can have an impact on how the company does its business.

Telephone contact with the customer reinforces the personal nature of caring about them. A letter should not only include the written apology for the specific cause of their complaint, and the written offer of compensation or remedy, but perhaps also an indication of how the customer's experience has resulted in some sort of on-going improvement in the quality of service provided. The final touch is for the manager to whom the complaint was originally referred to telephone the customer again about a week after they should have received the letter. This call is to check that all is in order and that the customer is satisfied with the outcome. This is one of the main contacts that actually builds the relationship and customer loyalty.

An essential feature of a service is that there is a relationship established between supplier and customer. Whilst mistakes should obviously be avoided, it is interesting to note that customers can be more satisfied and loyal if a mistake is resolved appropriately than if a mistake had not been made in the first place. The relationship has been developed because of the problem, and resolving the problem has taken the relationship on to a more personal and involved level. Conversely, customers who complain and feel that their grievance was not properly remedied can feel personally insulted because they have not been treated as individuals. The consequence of this will be loss of company reputation and probable loss of business, spread as far as the dissatisfied customer takes it.

Anyone who comes into contact with customers and who does not naturally possess the sort of 'people skills' necessary for dealing with complaints will find their job very hard to do, unless they receive positive guidance and tuition in techniques, as well as support, designed to help them cope with this dimension of their job. Specialist training for all staff likely to deal with a customer complaint is invariably cost-effective, helping the company to market its services at a profit. It is generally recognized in business

Be civil, not servile…

that the cost of gaining one new customer is five or six times greater than the cost of selling to an existing customer.

The service provider has to have a good working knowledge of the legal and/or ethical framework within which the service is supplied, and ensure that legal and ethical obligations are complied with. Consumer legislation is embodied in a raft of Acts of Parliament such as the Trade Descriptions Act 1968, Unfair Contract Terms Act 1977, Sale of Goods Act 1979, Sale and Supply of Goods Act 1994, Unfair Terms in Consumer Contracts Regulations 1994, and any subsequent amendments to such Acts. Consumer law is a complex area that is constantly changing. For example, consumers' remedies and rights are strengthened by EU directives, such as the Sale of Goods and Associated Guarantees Directive, that can have a bearing on how retailers handle certain complaints.

Complaints should be handled consistently, with persistent complaints being corrected at the fundamental level. Comprehensive records of customer complaints enable their swift resolution and corrective action to be formulated by management. Complaints and their resolution should be openly discussed and shared at management meetings so that any emerging patterns or trends can be highlighted and promptly dealt with.

KEY POINTS

- All contact from customers is to be welcomed, and this most definitely includes complaints.
- If only a 'damage limitation exercise' is undertaken in response to complaints, an excellent opportunity to create a loyal customer has been missed.
- The first thing to do with complainants is to listen attentively and then acknowledge their feelings.
- Empathize with them and offer an apology for the company having caused them distress.
- Speak in a low, calm voice without being defensive.
- Lead the customer aside for a more detailed review of the facts.
- Confirm the facts. Establish the real cause of dissatisfaction.
- Ask the customer how they would like the situation to be remedied.
- Provide the remedy on the spot if this is applicable. It may only require a sincere apology. Refund money if this will be accepted.
- If the complaint needs to be referred, it must go upwards before it can go sideways.
- The referring manager should take ownership of the complaint and follow it through the system.
- The customer should be told details of the procedure that is being adopted.
- Apart from taking accurate notes of the complaint, all other paperwork can be done after the customer has gone.
- A vital part of customer care is demonstrating that the individual customer can have an impact on the way the company operates.
- Telephoning the customer after two days reinforces the belief that the company cares about its customers.
- A letter of apology and compensation or remedy should follow within a week, also stating how the company has modified the way it does things to prevent a similar incident.
- The referring manager should telephone about a week later to check that the customer is satisfied.

- Customers can become more loyal if a mistake has been rectified, than if no complaint had occurred.
- Finding a new customer is at least five times more costly than selling to an existing customer.
- Consumer law is constantly changing and management must be sure to fulfil their legal and/or ethical obligations.
- To be able to fulfil this role, staff need to be well supported, trained and motivated.
- Complaints should be tracked and reviewed collectively so that management can correct persistent or emerging problems.

ACTION POINTS

- Review you customer complaints procedures.
- Arrange for necessary management and staff training.
- Obtain guidelines to the law set out in layman's terms.
- Build customer complaints follow ups and their review into the management agenda.
- Phone a customer who has recently complained. Make notes. Take action.

8

The marketing audit for service providers

A marketing audit is a systematic information-gathering process that highlights clearly where an organization stands along a scale ranging from no marketing to total sophistication. Its purpose is to give clear guidelines to management on how to improve current activities and to indicate possible development areas for the future. It is an analytical tool for: Evaluation, Measurement, Motivation, and Action.

Some of the areas covered in the following audit may not be applicable for some businesses as an attempt has been made to make it as comprehensive as possible. Your own action planning and prioritizing notes should be made as you progress through the audit, which is presented here in a summarized checklist format, divided into nine major sections:

- Your company;
- The market;
- Market research and market intelligence;
- Sales and sales administration;
- Sales force;
- Communications;
- Service range;
- Purchasing;
- Finance.

YOUR COMPANY

Corporate objectives

☐ Vision statement (the long term aim of the company): Is it written down in no more than two sentences? Has it (or part of it) been published? Are staff aware of the overall corporate objective? Do staff have clear, identifiable, realistic and achievable goals? Are customers aware of the company's stated overall objective?

☐ Mission Statement (how the company intends to achieve its vision): Is it written down and expressed in no more than one sentence? Are staff aware of it? Are customers informed of it?

☐ Markets in which a major presence is required: identified and listed?

☐ Allied markets that may represent profitable expansion areas: identified and listed?

☐ New markets to be exploited: identified and listed?

☐ Plans for merger, partnership, acquisition, joint venture, or other strategic alliance: identified and considered?

☐ Plans for future agency, distributorship, etc: identified and considered?

☐ Financial objectives – profit, turnover, ROCE, balance sheet strength, gearing, etc: details identified and intermediate targets set?

☐ Planned pace and direction of business growth: defined and stated?

☐ Planned 'exit' strategy? For the owner manager? From declining markets? For the company as a whole in its present form?

Corporate strategy

☐ Strategic summary of planned pace and direction of business growth?

☐ Policy on required corporate image?

☐ Naming, design, style, presentation to the various 'stakeholders' and 'public'?

☐ Financial control, funding, stringencies, reports? Use of existing assets?

☐ IT strategies; Internet presence?
☐ Service development/diversification; market development?
☐ Personnel management, training, incentives, etc?

Corporate long range operating plan

☐ Broad methods by which the corporate objectives will be achieved in terms of: marketing, sales, service distribution, finance, suppliers, and administrative control?
☐ Procedures for updating corporate operating plans: for review, monitoring and control of information input, analysis, interpretation and action?

THE MARKET

☐ Make-up by market sectors, by sizes and other market distinctions?
☐ Analysis of market competitors in each sector by company/brand share ranking?
☐ Trends based on past history; changes brought about by technical advances, movements dictated by facility availability and/or prices, distribution changes, etc?
☐ Client/customer attitudes, their purchasing and usage habits; decision makers and influencers?
☐ Effects of government actions, political and/or legal factors, social changes, local and national economic factors?
☐ Pricing structures and their levels through market histories?
☐ Major communications (advertising) methods, trends, changes?
☐ Service Life Cycle curves: current position of market for each sector/segment, duration before expected change; limiting factors?

MARKET RESEARCH AND MARKET INTELLIGENCE

☐ Ongoing internal systems for gathering, analysing and interpreting market data?
☐ Regular provision for continuing market assessment from published reports and statistics; history; methods and costs?

☐ Specially commissioned studies with limited or general circulation; reports and/or analyses, and their costs?

☐ Overseas research reports of relevance to own markets?

☐ Research reports on specific aspects such as usage, attitudes, motivation, psychology, preference, advertising/promotional effectiveness?

☐ Marketing 'steers' to technical researching suggesting lines of enquiry relative to perceived market trends?

☐ Results of own test marketing activities and results of competitors' activities?

☐ Research budgets; relationship to overall marketing budgets and, where possible, to turnover?

SALES AND SALES ADMINISTRATION

☐ Unit sales, with breakdowns for each market sector: by geographic region, customer/client type, service type, etc?

☐ Turnover history of service range at 'current' and 'stable' prices, in total, and by major service type and market sectors/segments?

☐ Relationship of sales to forecasts and targets. Methods of forecasting, bases used, accuracy expected?

☐ Establishment of targets for sales and sales administration. Methods of origination, control, notification. Are targets based on forecasts and are both the same as objectives? Are there separate forecasts for sales and finance?

☐ Methods and accuracy of sales analyses; service values, cancellations, additions, errors, 'branded' or specially presented services?

☐ Use of IT as an analytical tool? Construction and upkeep of customer/sales databases?

☐ 'Delivery' analysis by: size of account sale, customer/client type, area, administrative processing time?

☐ Sales processing procedure, checks, action with enquiries and complaints?

☐ Sales to call ratio, sales value per customer/client, average sales size?

☐ Market shares, by company/brand and service group, for self and competitors, in both sterling value and number of unit sales?

SALES FORCE

- [ ] Structure and organization, with changes in operation, responsibilities, calling patterns. Use of telephone canvassing, telephone selling, agents, distributors, etc?
- [ ] Extent of e-commerce strategies?
- [ ] Personnel, with changes in numbers, location, job specification?
- [ ] Methods of incentive, commission, bonuses, employee share options, promotions, in cash, in perks' and in kind?
- [ ] Journey cycles, routing methods, time spent selling related to: total customer/client relationship, administration, 'merchandising', research, travelling, etc?
- [ ] Customer/client relationship service (after-sales and on-going care); organization; reputation?
- [ ] 'Merchandising' methods, personnel, effectiveness?
- [ ] Sales reports, method, frequency, content, level of analysis 'in the field', new ideas and suggestions, transmission/discussion?
- [ ] Methods of selling, use of call cards, notebook/laptop computers?
- [ ] Use of price lists, brochures, literature, display material, audio-visual aids?
- [ ] Cost to the marketing budget, as opposed to the sales budget, of printed material, aids promotions, joint advertising, exhibition representations, etc?
- [ ] Customer/client correspondence and personal communication, handling and reporting procedure. Access to legal advice?
- [ ] Recording of inter-group or inter-division sales?
- [ ] System for provision of quotations, estimates, proposals, specifications, tenders, speculative presentations, costs, etc. Drawing up terms and conditions of contract?
- [ ] Sales conferences: why, when, where, duration, formats, contribution required from marketing?
- [ ] Training: in-company and external, method, frequency, effectiveness, progression, costs?

COMMUNICATIONS

- [ ] Sales promotion history, successes and failures, methods of measurement?

☐ Promotional activity within each sector, by service and by target customer group. Cost effectiveness?

☐ The extent to which promotional pricing activity has affected recognized standard returns?

☐ Direct mail: use, costs and effectiveness for each service and each target customer group. Use of direct mail lists; list management; response rates?

☐ Public relations activity (rarely measurable in sales terms). Corporate activity?

☐ Presence at exhibitions, trade fairs, conferences, seminars; usefulness, costs?

☐ Literature such as brochures, proposals, notices, news sheets, etc. Display material purpose: use, effectiveness, for special promotional activity or regular business, exhibitions, conferences, seminars, etc?

☐ Media advertising history. Media used and tested: costs, effectiveness. Media production costs, original artwork, copyright, relationship between 'above the line' and 'below the line'. Media budgets, method of origination, past history at constant prices, relationship to sales, to attitude changes, to market 'shifts'?

☐ Relationship to competitors' advertising and promotional activity? Integration of own total communications programmes with media specials, industry or special customer requirements?

☐ Use of outside agencies: advertising, sales promotion, research, design, media buying, creative, public relations, marketing, telecanvassing, merchandising, direct mail, Web site designers/managers, exhibitions, etc. Responsibilities and costs?

☐ Origination of strategies, particularly sales promotion and advertising. Who originates, how controlled, what changes, and why?

☐ Overall integration of communications: are they all coherent?

☐ Legal constraints and controls, responsibilities and monitoring methods?

SERVICE RANGE

☐ Brand name(s): method of presentation, relationship to other company names. Printing specifications: name, logo, contents, legality?

☐ Specifications, descriptions of service types/uses, contents of targeted 'packages', changes to these over time?

☐ Market research and development programmes for future changes?

☐ New service introductions, launches, innovations, withdrawals?

☐ Trade marks, licences, warrantees/guarantees involved, legal constraints?

☐ Sources of design work, corporate literature, Web site design and associated technology?

☐ Industry and customer awareness, attitudes, image, usage of services, ease of use?

☐ All of the above for competitors, together with comparative data?

☐ Sources of data for own services and competitors, with degree of accuracy, frequency and topicality?

☐ Administrative capacity; relationship to proportion of overheads, etc?

PURCHASING

☐ Methods of ordering consumables, equipment replacements, additions and maintenance?

☐ Methods of ordering design work and print work; any promotional services; legal clearances, etc?

☐ Lead times required for all of the above?

☐ Relationship between sales forecast, revenue requirements, and purchasing. Methods of deciding on quantities?

☐ Duration of purchase/lease contracts; relationships with suppliers?

☐ Quality control of inward supplies, methods and action?

☐ Basis of decision making concerning suppliers?

☐ Procedure on cost control; ability to keep up-to-date with prices, technological innovation, suppliers?

☐ Methods of advising problems on delivery, price, quality, etc?

☐ Liaison with marketing, sales force, finance?

FINANCE

☐ Turnover history of service range, at 'current' and 'stable' prices, in total, and by major sectors of service type and customer type?

☐ Profit history, gross and net before tax, relative to turnover?

☐ Financial contribution similarly analysed?

☐ Relevant profit ratios for marketing: profit to turnover, turnover to marketing budgets, etc?

☐ Reasons for changes in above records?

☐ Source of funding expansion; availability of working capital?

☐ Internal bookkeeping transactions across profit centres?

☐ Price history in terms of average turnover, with relationship to inflation, competitors' prices, service development; with reasons for changes?

☐ Price structures. Standard charges, discounts, advertising allowances, etc. Increases on previous year?

☐ Costs records in terms of supplies, administration, selling, servicing accounts, customer research and development, marketing?

☐ Marketing budget breakdowns in total, and separately for such relevant items as, advertising, sales promotion, printing, research, salaries, training and personnel development, etc?

References and further reading

Branson, R (2000) *Losing My Virginity*, Virgin Publishing, London

Kotler, P and Armstrong, G (1991) *Principles of Marketing*, 5th edn, Prentice-Hall, Englewood Cliffs, NJ

Mintel Marketing Intelligence (2000) Automated finances, the ATM and kiosk, in *Finance Intelligence*, Mintel International Group Limited, London

Ulver (1987) *Do Not Ask the Price: Memoirs of the President of Marks and Spencer*, Ulverscroft

Index